"Martignetti hungers for one thing in all his stories: truth—however absurd, painful, or wonderful it may be. His characters shine with the unmistakable spark of humanity, and by the end of the collection feel as real as that old friend, or rival, or torturer in our own lives. The difference is, after rolling through the waves of hurt, laughter and love in these powerful stories, we see them—and ourselves—more clearly than when we began."

—*Ana Hebra Flaster*

Commentator, NPR's All Things Considered
Contributor, *The Boston Globe* and *Boston Globe Magazine*

"These beautiful stories invite us into tender, uncertain settings; they grip the heart, and then leave us redeemed through a fuller embrace of our flawed humanity.

Anthony Martignetti abides in a courageous, compassionate place where most of us forget we actually live."

—*Christopher Germer*, PhD

Author, *The Mindful Path to Self-Compassion*

"In Anthony Martignetti's stories, every word is as urgent as a suicide."

—*Steven Bogart*

Guest Director, American Repertory Theater
Artist in Residence, Southern New Hampshire
University.

"It's a mad, mad world in Anthony Martignetti's *Lunatic Heroes*, a 1950s and 60s childhood presided over by a pantheon of familial deities ranging from the ditzy to the deranged. Martignetti's tales are 'thick with the smear and scent' of a time gone by—a world somehow resurrected and burnished with the author's affection, honesty, and ardent memory. A revelation!"

—*Chip Hartranft*

Translator of *The Yoga-Sutra of Patañjali.*

Lunatic Heroes
Memories, Lies and Reflections

C. Anthony Martignetti

INTRODUCTION BY AMANDA PALMER

3 SWALLYS PRESS
BOSTON, MASSACHUSETTS, USA

Paperback ISBN 978-0-9882300-0-2

1-Memoir 2-Literature

To Keno, Bullfrog, Carl, Ray, Stevie D.,
Jackie, Joe, Nonno, Mikee, Carol, Joey,
and all the Lunatic Heroes who have
lived and died with me.

Thank you for saving me within an inch of my life.

Acknowledgements

I want to thank Amanda Palmer, whose long friendship, regular encouragement, support, and confidence led to the creation of this book. We were at a bar in Boston a couple of years ago when she said, "I really love your stories, and you need to get them out." I said, "Yeah, ok."

Knowing that I was just saying that to placate her, she said, "You have to want to do it or it won't happen. *I will help you.*" I think it was the earnestness with which she spoke those last four words that started a shift.

Then, she married Neil Gaiman, and I became so jealous of his raging success and amazing stories that I decided to actually give it a shot.

My friend, Nivi Nagiel, who has walked through every step of this process with me . . . each word, comma and "agoog." She has made me feel these stories are worth sharing and she never, ever lies, due to a constitutional incapacity. She would very much like to lie, but simply cannot. Also, she loves me despite knowing me.

Paul Trainor, my mucker, all around great talent and the entire IT team. His reading, editing, designing and energizing this book was deeply needed and is appreciated. When we part, he's always saying to me, "Be lucky." I got really lucky when we met and became friends.

Shawna McCarthy, who was sent by an American God to edit these stories. I think she liked them.

The Souled Out Artists writers' group, for their help and collaboration, and out of which many of these stories emerged.

And, as always, the bottom line, my wife, Laura Sanford, who encourages me in all things. Without doubt, she is the best person I've ever known at loving. And the only one I can imagine who would stay married to me for twenty-seven years. Thank you, my dearest dear.

Thanks to all of you who have listened to me read stories over the years and urged me to do more with them . . . and to those erudite friends who endorsed this collection with their blurbs.

With you, I am more than nothing.

C. Anthony Martignetti, 2012

Lunatic Heroes
Memories, Lies and Reflections

Contents

Introduction

Anthony moved in next door when I was nine. He was in his thirties.

I've been trying, since then, to explain to people exactly WHAT he was (and is) to me. He wasn't quite my friend, wasn't quite my parent, wasn't quite my teacher.

I usually fumbled around describing him to people by mumbling the words "mentor," "guru," "best friend," but mostly found myself satisfied with this particular run-on: "Anthony moved in next door when I was nine and taught me everything I know about love and knows me better than anybody and we still talk almost every single day even if I'm in Japan," variations of which I still use when trying to describe a relatively indescribable relationship.

He loves telling the story of one of the first interactions we had, soon after he moved in. It was a winter night, after a big snowfall in our little suburban neighborhood, and he and his wife were hosting a dinner party.

I ambled across my lawn over to his and started

pelting his window with snowballs. I thought it was funny. He sort of did too.

He came to the door.

"I want a snowball fight," I said.

"I can't," he said. "But I'll get you back later."

And he returned to the dinner party, back into the warmth and fire and wine of the adult world behind him.

Then, according to the story, I returned to his house about twenty minutes later, and started pelting their giant picture window with snowballs for a second time.

He came to the door again. "What the hell?"

"You said you'd get me later," I said. "I'm here to get gotten."

"Amanda, it's been twenty minutes," he said. "I meant later... like... tomorrow."

I don't actually remember this happening. But I know the story by heart, because he's told it so many times.

I also don't actually remember the first time I hugged him, but he tells that story too.

I was probably fourteen by that time, and our relationship had evolved from occasional snowball enemies to full-on pals.

He claims we were standing in his driveway and something had happened that merited a hug. But we had never hugged and I was, according to him, into the idea...

but wasn't used to hugging. So I leaned my body against his, he says, like a falling pine tree, letting my head rest on his chest while my body kept a terrified distance.

Anthony is a therapist, and a good listener.

I needed someone to listen. And we went to town on each other.

Everything that happened to me through my angst-ridden teen and college years, he heard it all: the sex, the drugs, the boyfriends, the break-ups, the depression, the anger, the identity crises. He listened. He took dozens of phone calls in the middle of the night during anxiety attacks, boyfriend and girlfriend fights, drunken terrors. From Germany, I called collect from the phone booth down the street at three in the morning. He racked up thousand dollar phone bills when I lived far from home. He advised, he dropped hints, but he never judged. He never reprimanded, and he never gave me an ultimatum (with one exception: the time I brought home a junkie boyfriend. When I did that, he made some relatively strong suggestions.).

He never told me what to do. Instead, he told me stories.

Stories about his life, stories about Zen masters, stories about his father, stories about his grandfather, stories about old farmers. This was one of my favorites:

A farmer is sitting on his porch in a chair, hanging out with his dog.

A friend walks up to the porch to say hello, and hears an awful yelping, squealing sound coming from the dog.

"What's the matter with Ol' Blue?" asks the friend.

"He's layin' on a nail that's pokin' up from the floorboards," says the farmer.

"Why doesn't he just sit up and get off it?" asks the friend.

The farmer deliberates on this and replies: "Don't hurt enough yet."

I carried that story with me through heartbreak after heartbreak, and through giant, painful, personal transitions. And I've since re-told it to many friends and advice-seekers. The general moral: When it truly hurts enough... you eventually move your ass.

Here's another of my favorites:

A Zen student walks into his master's chamber. The student is shocked and appalled to see that the Zen master is drinking his morning tea out of a treasured, priceless Ming-dynasty teacup belonging to the monastery.

"How can you do this?" asks the student. "This teacup is a priceless treasure. What if it falls? What if it breaks?"

The Zen master smiles and says: "I consider it already broken."

He regaled me with tales from the sixties that made my heart yearn and pound to turn back the clock and live in a time when everybody hitchhiked and smoked hash while listening to rock 'n roll. He drew pictures of wild kids creating a new reality and paradigm in an upheaved world, running around with feathers in their hair and knives in their boots, terrorizing the system and trying to score as many girls, joints, and adventures as they could.

Anthony was raised in a big Italian-American family who'd made their fortune in the liquor and real estate business. His whole network of brothers and sisters and cousins reminded me of The Godfather. His weird combination of a calm, Buddhist approach to life (he taught and introduced me to yoga, meditation, and the general concept of mindfulness) and the facts that he had a black belt in Karate, would arm me with pepper spray before I went on long trips alone, and had an arsenal of bizarre, conventional and esoteric self-defense weapons in his therapist's office never struck me as strange. I recently realized that in my Hollywood biopic, he'd be Mr. Miagi from the Karate Kid but played by Robert De Niro. In a critical over-dramatic scene in the film, I would tell him that I'd been raped by a boy from school. He would then narrow his eyes, make an Italian gesture in which he bit his folded tongue in half while wrinkling his nose and say, calmly: "I'm going to find that guy and beat his ass," then he'd put his hands in yoga prayer position over his heart, bow his head and add: "...with compassion."

We used to talk about what would happen when he died. I worried about it. He's more than twenty years older than me. It seemed inevitable. I once asked him what I should do at his funeral, since probably I'd have to say something.

He gave this some thought. He said he'd like me to walk up to the front of the room, carrying a stick from a tree outside.

"Don't say anything," he requested. "Just hold that sucker up in the air, break it in half, and throw it on the floor."

Everything breaks.

We shared our stories on the phone, in long letters, sometimes typewritten, sometimes handwritten, and eventually over email. In person, on long walks, over food, over tea, over coffee, over wine. Over years and years.

As I got older, he shared more and more of the real things. Not just the entertaining stories, but the sad ones. The scary ones. The mean ones. The shocking ones.

Meanwhile, I wrote songs. I tried to make them as honest as I could. I got better and better at being less afraid to share the terrifying. We egged each other on.

Our ability to share our darknesses made us lighter. And through all this, we hugged. As much as needed, close and unafraid.

Then he started writing some of his stories down, for real. I can't remember when. I was maybe in my twenties. I didn't think much of it at the time. We'd always written long, detailed letters, and while email sort of killed our letter-writing habits, the fact that he would commit some of his tales to legit, short-story form didn't seem like much of a stretch. I loved reading his stories, it wasn't as good as hearing them in person, but it was a close second. He spent more time, dug deeper, pulled out details that he didn't on walks and over food, because he had more time to sprinkle in subtler shades and shape the background. Eventually, he started reading them to groups of people. And more people. And then, one day, I told him he should publish the stories. Actually, I didn't tell him he *should*, I told him he *had to*.

It was a few years ago, and we were sitting in a loud, dark bar in Boston, drinking beer. I hadn't meant to bring it up, but the conversation turned to his pile of stories, which he'd been reading aloud as part of a writing group that occasionally held events to share their work.

"You know you have to publish all the stories," I said. "You have enough of them. And they're really, really fucking good. And I'll help."

And so, slowly and slightly reluctantly, he started.

Shortly after that day, a few months later, I was on the fifth day of an off-line yoga retreat with my sister, about 4,000 miles from home.

Anthony hadn't been feeling well before I left, he'd had a crazy spell in the hospital with a rare affliction, but it hadn't been fatal and he was going through a battery of tests.

I got the text one afternoon when I took a break from yoga-solitude and oasis, and turned my cell phone on to check for emergencies. The doctors had given him six months, tops.

It was over, the story was closing.

I entered a state of total shock and called Neil, my writer husband. He knew what Anthony meant to me. He heard the news, heard my tone of voice, and went to work to get me on the next plane out of dodge.

Before I left the retreat, I went to the woods and grabbed a stick.

The trip back to Boston involved three flights and took about twenty-six hours. When I got to the first big airport, I walked catatonically into a news shop and bought a blank book. And I started writing. Every thing I could think of that Anthony had ever told me, every piece of advice, every skit we'd made up together, every memory. Every single story. If I stopped writing and started thinking about the reality of losing him, I'd weep, so I kept the pen to the paper and didn't stop. The ink flowing to the blank pages of that book was my lifeline, my IV, my only escape from collapsing. In that moment, I understood something about my writer husband that I'd never understood before. I had a small glimpse into the act of writing as a direct escape from pain. For the first time, I experienced the physical truth of what it felt like to dwell in the act of creation as the only viable escape from an unbearable, unfaceable reality.

A few weeks later, second opinions were bounced around. The death sentence lifted.

We still don't know how much time we have with each other.... but we never do, do we?

The stories you will read in this book are a collection of confabulated memories. Most of it is true, some of it isn't, but the emotional truth never lies.

To lift up the dank, heavy carpet and show you the grime, dried blood and crushed bugs underneath: that is the act that I aspire to every day. Anthony and his stories have been a huge ingredient in my own ability to do so. What you find under there is never pretty, but the act of lifting the carpet is—in itself—an act of salvation.

We help each other lift. Anthony was my personal trainer for years, teaching me how to use my frail muscles to pull up the carpet, even when it was water-logged and heavy as steel. For this, I owe him— quite literally—my life. I've made a career and entire artistic empire out of the act of lifting up that carpet... and

I don't plan on stopping anytime soon.

My arms are flexed and ready.

When the day comes, I'll get up at his funeral and break a giant stick.

Then I'll head to a bar and spend the rest of the night drinking, laughing, crying... and waiting to die.

Somebody bring a stick.

—Amanda Palmer
New York City
June 26th, 2012

Force Fed

"Your father is a good man, and he will rip the skin off your face if you don't eat this," my grandmother snarled as she mimed the procedure on her own face. Her left arm dangled by her side, a remnant of a stroke at age forty-nine, which also left her face in a heartrending but twisted freaky-smile. With the tilting limp and cane, diabetes and obesity mixed in, she was a grim character. This decent woman was never attractive a day in her life, but now, unsightly was the best you could give her. When I told my father

My grandmother and me

1

what his mother had said, he replied that she wouldn't say anything like that and besides he would never hurt me, and what's the matter with me that I could think such a thing anyway.

You just want to bite yourself.

Between four and ten years old, the "eat /not eat" question was the central issue of my life and why my family staged scene after scene around forcing food into me.

No one could have referred to me as a chow-hound when I was a kid. I was stem-skinny and stood out among my fat relatives; which included obese paternal grandparents, great aunts and uncles, regular aunts and uncles, and their offspring—a cluster of chubby children who were depressing examples of our nation's current "epidemic." They'd all stagger into kitchens, lumbering past me like circus elephants on morphine and honk into the food as if every day was the one before lent. They could eat through a pantry like a cloud of grasshoppers.

Not me. Going with little food wasn't a big deal. I wasn't hungry, and just couldn't get much of it down. It was a genuine case of anorexia (not *anorexia nervosa*, so popular and alluring today, but simply reduced appetite), especially when faced with what I considered to be completely gross. And all things revolting were customary fare in my father's family and not eating them

Two little kids from the
neighborhood and me

was a sin. My grand-mother taught us to kiss rock-hard, mold-speckled bread before we threw it away. Food was sacred.

Now, I don't think it's terribly strange for a kid to have food preferences and to be cautious when it comes to putting things in one's mouth. But, with respect to that view, I was alone. I was alone, it seemed, most of the time. My father, uncles and grandfather were at work six days a week. Nobody was around, nobody really knew. They would have been appalled and angry if they were to witness the way I was being treated. They were good men . . . of this, I am sure.

Mealtime options were often strange—especially the nasty, smelly, spicy, eccentric Southern Italian stuff they dished-up at various family gatherings, including, but not limited to: whole roasted goat-head (with boiled eyes wide open, trapped in lidless terror and conveying a silent curse to those gathered at the table), pigs' feet, congealed blood pie, baby cow stomachs still brimming with the mother's milk from its last meal (this was boiled whole

3

and eaten out of the stomach-lining), and astringent, bitter greens. Worst of all was the *formaggio marcio*, cheese, purposely containing live maggots, which leapt and frolicked on the plate in celebration when the first liberating wedge was cut out. This is wrong on so many levels. Garlic, garlic, and more garlic, garlic out your butt. Raw garlic is strong stuff, but its reported powers to keep vampires away is bullshit. Rare lamb-chops (something about lambs), soft-boiled eggs sitting upright in special cups oozing gelatinous embryonic juice. Raw parsley on nearly everything, oregano on everything else, slick calves' liver (for the love of God, a liver . . . why don't you just plop a throbbing heart on the plate?), chalky, rubbery, raw spinach, tough, furry, half-cooked string beans, and anchovies (as we know these are hairy fish gone bad). And to begin the day, if I dodged the runny eggs, there was clumpy oatmeal, and freakin' Wheatina. These were followed by heaping tablespoons of cod liver oil, which coated the mouth and throat with slime and left me, for the first couple of periods in school, with breath like a mackerel.

This was all throw-up food. But you learn to keep things in.

Inexplicably, many of the adults saw my position regarding the more conventional of these items as resistance, petulance, and defiance, and perhaps it was. I have no clue what I was feeling beyond a weak appetite and a strong desire to avoid eating half-formed farm animals and their entrails.

At the kitchen table in my grandparents' home, on one of those many days I was left there to be looked after, barely able to face the food staring back at me from my plate, grandmother misshapen and slouching over me (she smelled fleshy, in a necrotic way, a perfume of illness and insulin). I am reeling from aroma and anxiety and I have to eat the food—I want to be sick, but I have to eat it—because from the rooms above there is a tremendous banging – *BOOM – BOOM – BOOM – BOOM!* The ancient house resounds as if being whacked by a wrecking-ball, shuddering me, and the whole place to the foundations. *BOOM! BOOM!* The noise smashed through the tension amplifying it to intolerable levels. Again, *BOOM, BOOM, BOOM!*

Shock turns to panic and fright. My grandmother asks ominously, *Hah? Do you know what that is? That's Father Romano's sister coming down from upstairs, she lives in the attic, and if you don't eat she will get you and choke you and then she's gonna kill you.* I cry, I shake. How could this be happening? I need help. I'm scared . . . I'm facing death by putrid food or death at the hands of a ghoul. One, you die puking, the other, screaming. Nauseous or terrified, you buy the farm either way.

Father Romano's sister, this gorgon, I am informed, is enormous, with long stringy hair and huge feet.

I figure I better get gulping.

I half-choke down and part vomit up what I had just swallowed in my blubbering attempt to fend off execution by the monster lumbering in my direction. ***BOOM*** . . . it doesn't stop . . . ***BOOM***. I am delirious with the noise, my grandmother's broken-English demands, her good fist pounding on the table causing the dead arm to jiggle lifeless by her side, the churning stomach, the gag-drool, the eternal dread. ***Eat!***

The attic sound effects, I learned much later, were from my great aunts slamming chairs on the floor in the rooms above the kitchen. These recently imported relatives stood as certifiable midgets, but on the farm in southern Italy from which they hailed, they likely exceeded average height. They were both good women, as was, my father regularly informed me, my grandmother. The older great aunt is long gone, and the younger, always my favorite, and an early source of welcome but practically inconsequential compassion, is now ninety-nine. These miniscule women were put to their duplicitous task by the eldest sister, my grandmother, in a loving effort to shock me toward nutrition.

I was a little boy alternately crying, choking, hyperventilating, nauseous, desperate, and helpless. I envied the dead.

I wasn't launching any revolt, not making a statement—being obstinate or obstreperous—I didn't eat because I couldn't. I would have if I could have. I would have done anything to steer clear of the terror train coming for me. I would have eaten myself just to disappear. And then were the assured punishments from my mother, Jackie, that awaited me back at my parents' apartment once the news got there that, again, I had resisted food.

Back home in the small, near empty flat, I was punished because my mother had fallen victim to the paralyzing fear of presenting a bad image ("Mala Figura," the elders would say). *"Your son, he doesn't eat. He's skinny, he looks sick, like you—if he doesn't eat that means You Are A Bad Mother. He should be fat like his cousins. We got money…we made it in this country…we don't have T.B., but you and your son, you make us look bad. And you, you're starved like a mezzo-morto (half dead). You bring disgrace to the family."*

And my mother—the foolish child of the mirror— she, the unschooled, untutored, ill from anxiety, believed them. And so, she beat me. She beat me to make me eat. She nearly killed me in place of Father Romano's sister. She beat me to burnish the gloss on her image . . . punishing me to make her look good . . . to the elders, the in-laws, the butchers, who chopped and chopped to break the bones of my will . . . and they did. Sort of.

She did her best, my mother. She tried. She tried to be good. She didn't realize the impact on me. Why? I don't know to this day, why. Except to say that her narcissism and fragility could bear no criticism.

Just to fill in a gap: Father Romano had been a frequent visitor to my grandparents' home. He attended large family events, there as "The Priest." You had to have one, and often a nun as well. Our nun was Sister Mary Agnes, my father's grammar school teacher, whom he blindly venerated for all of his life, and had over to our house every few years for dinner. She was nice enough I guess, but seemed almost unreal and sort of ridiculous in her enormous medieval garb. She swished around with a grandeur that held us in thrall, was exceedingly tall with black lace-up heels and a starched white and black head dress rising a good six to eight inches above her freckled brow. My mother ran around holding her breath all night, obsequious and servile, as if in the presence of a living deity. My father was even worse, becoming a total lamb around her, bleating through the evening. He did everything but lick her lily-white hands clean after she finished dinner. We had a nun; my grandparents, a priest.

Father Romano was the priest in tenure to my grandparents, and from Italy; my image has him always in a full-length, grease-stained cassock and Roman collar, which served as a firm base to support an enormous bald head on his slightly hunched body. He carried himself in the humble and pious way only priests back then could pull off.

The old black and white family photo albums are replete with pictures of him—each image the same no matter the surroundings, the other guests, or the year taken. As if Photoshopped into each gathering, he lurked like a statue: same outfit, same posture, same expression. He was fixed, unalterable. Like Nosferatu.

Father Romano, Uncle Fred, me, and Auntie Millie

He emanated a musty and cryptic scent, perhaps from the white circular salt stains around the underarms of his black robe. His eyebrows, stiff as wires, jutted out like the brim of a fedora. He was already ancient when I first knew him. To me, he was a spook. Period.

Though my mother remembered him as a "good man," he freaked me out. And, of course, the very thought of his deranged and hideous garret-dwelling sister was unbearable. Let's face it, if he was related to her, if he spent his childhood around her, he probably had a hand in making her that way. He could very well have been the Frankenstein behind the monster for all I knew, and maybe he had turned to God to make up for his heinous misdeeds . . . how good could he be?

I just couldn't fit all the fear into the five-year-old head bobbing on my soon-to-be-strangled neck. But enough dread got in to make me gag down the grotesque, google-eyed mish-mash in front of me.

And so I ate and cried, vomited and heaved and became sicker and skinnier and Father Romano's sister became larger and stronger until I was no match for her. So I quit—checked out—threw in the napkin—evaporated into my thoughts and fantasies and dreamed. And I changed. In my dreams, terror turned into excitement, and fear into consolation. I wasn't there in the same way any longer. In my dreams, She-Devils compelled me, Sirens dragged me to their festivals to torment me, punish me, and I ached to attend—I joined them, became an eager guest on their hot and wicked shores. This was my boyish odyssey . . . my search to find peace and solace, and to avoid being hacked to death by the cleavers of shame and control.

*See, you can't frighten me . . . you aren't torturing me
. . . I like it; you're doing what I want you to do. You're
exciting me: BOOMBOOMBOOM? . . . Who's upstairs now?*

If only there were some conscious strategy or
strength in it . . . but there was no such thing. That is
just another idea, another dream. All I felt was guilt and
embarrassment for my sinful fantasies. I escaped, yes . . .
but I ran to a forbidden place to do it. I ran to where the
priests said men go when they turn from God and to the
Devil. I ran toward the deluding ecstasy of defeat. I ran
away, sprinting to a hell of my own making. A hell I
could control.

Despite this massive inner shift, I became, around
this time, unwell and even more repelled by many things
beyond the menu items. All of an egg, if it wasn't
cooked to shoe leather, terrified me: shell, yolk, white.
The smell of drinking glasses and cutlery, which to me
carried odors of egginess and raw meat. Any meat which
showed signs of blood repelled me. I reeled from the
queasy smell of hard cheeses and the moldy smell of the
soft ones. Even the hands of my female relatives
sickened me—their bleach-tinged hands—shiny and
reeking with chemicals. I couldn't bear them touching
me with those hands—those cracked and split hands and
fingers, painful and broken-open by the cares and chores
of dreary routine. I'd become frightened and revolted by
those gloomy hands and held my breath around them.

Hands looked slimy—bodies became as repellant as food had—I didn't want to be close to anyone, didn't want to be touched by anyone. It wasn't safe. I didn't have anything against anybody. I was just repulsed. I couldn't swallow them. My own flesh and blood.

It got to the point where I could smell everything, even from long distances. My olfactory sense became a primary protection, a gatekeeper, a firewall against threat—and these smells became actual tastes upon my tongue. I tasted locker rooms and hospital rooms. People's kitchens—I smelled, and tasted meals from those kitchens. I smelled people's breath from yards away. I could smell people's feet even in their shoes and socks. I smelled their hair and scalps and underarms—I smelled all their body odors; their skin surfaces and their bowels—their bloody meat and eggy innards.

All of it churned my stomach.

These sensations went farther when certain words became linked with the foods and bodies and smells, and those words I couldn't bear either. Words such as: *flesh* and *blood* and *spleen* and *nipple* and *slice* and *strip* and *split*—these were all cringe-worthy. I forced myself to bear them in public, holding my breath and clenching my jaw when they were spoken by others, but when alone I'd say them to myself compulsively, mechanically, over and over, and I'd shake and shudder and snap my neck and head—activities that others would notice had I been observed. But I avoided notice. It was unsafe to be seen.

I had to be mad in seclusion . . . a private lunacy in a solo asylum.

I wanted so much to be left alone. Alone and safe from the hands and the bodies and the food—safe from my family, safe from punishment and Father Romano's sister. I wanted to live in the trees or in my own apartment, where I, and only I, would prepare all the food and create all the smells and manage all the bodies, where all the flesh and blood would be protected, unblemished and unbruised.

I wanted fresh air, earth smells, sky and cloud smells, natural water, grass, the woods, the pond, laundry that had been hung outside smells. Outdoors felt safe to me in every season. The trees stood by not judging, not punishing, but passively protecting and sheltering. I felt secure with the small, wild animals in their silent awareness. Outside I was safe from bodies and foods— safe from penalty and from that furious, imprisoned sister. I wanted only to live in my fantasies unfettered. But fetters are part of the deal . . . everything comes with a price tagging along behind. Call it a cost of living fee.

I could find no deep or lasting refuge anywhere beyond my psychic retreat. Not in books, because I could not concentrate. I spent grammar school essentially reading the same few paragraphs over and over. Nor in religion, because my sinful, forbidden dreams and visions prevented me. Nothing took. I couldn't fit anything else in my head but my fantasies. As the child of Catholics, I had been in religious development since birth, and became an altar boy directly after having qualified for the sacraments of confession and communion. It was there they began the cheerful and beguiling chant, *Eat this for this is my flesh, drink this for this is my blood,* and that nearly put me around the bend with the shuddering and head-snapping, and though I was drawn, I was repelled, and though I needed spiritual nourishment just as I did bodily sustenance, I was unable to tolerate it.

Catholicism combined my two greatest concerns ("eating" and "bodies") and made those bizarre issues even more grotesque in the form of "eating a body." So here, my one shot at salvation as a Catholic required me to eat the animal flesh and drink the animal blood. I figured I was a goner; *In Nomine Patris, et Filii, et Spirtus Sancti.* Close the book on me!

Still, I began to imagine that, as in the religion I was being fed, perhaps the crucified are redeemed or that at the least the crucifiers eventually go to their victims to make amends, for their own salvation. And that maybe there was a chance to finally be safely seen, released, and made complete . . . helped.

As it turned out, this theory didn't hold for me. Help was not on the way.

So I had to bear day upon day of force-feeding of flesh and blood. Being force-fed doesn't mean so much that someone makes you *eat* a thing—it means that someone makes you *into* a thing.

And if there was any deliverance to be found in the brutality, it was that being made into a thing at least *you're* not red meat and *you* don't have a slimy center— you're safe from all that. You can become inanimate, inhuman.

For the record, there were things I did want to eat: peanut butter and jelly or Fluffernutter sandwiches for example, Chef Boyardee spaghetti and ravioli, corn flakes, hot dogs, beans and brown bread and some kinds of Chinese food on Saturday nights. I was even able to tolerate fish sticks and tartar sauce on Friday nights. I could handle well-done crispy chicken if it was unadulterated pure white meat. I liked corn, potatoes and peas (hated those Lc Sucur peas in a can though). I loved grape soda, pizza, gum, honey, maple sugar. I liked ice cream. I liked plums, pomegranates, persimmons and Hershey bars. What's wrong with all that?

That was more than five decades ago.

Now I eat (fruits and vegetables, mostly), and drink (water and wine, typically), and can be touched some.

I never managed to cultivate a taste for milk . . .

But the echoes of Father Romano's sister reverberate in the attics of my sleep. Her fast, loud footfalls come to get me still, to terrorize and kill me, rip the skin off my face, wring my neck and wrench the heart right out of me. Still, in darkness, beneath my covers, and the layers of years . . . still, she approaches:

BOOM BOOM BOOM

And the fear of punishment lingers in dark corridors—down from the attic, up from the grave, from inside the cathedral, from within my own body, which turns on itself—my grandmother, my mother, my family, my flesh, my blood.

Joe

By the time I was nine, we had left Medford for Lexington. "Moved to the sticks," as my grandparents, aunts and uncles called it. "What are they crazy? They're moving out to the sticks, for cry-eye," they'd say, even though it was actually only eight miles from our old house and only seven and a quarter from my grandparents. It was still the farthest out from town that anyone from the family had ever gone.

In this sense, my father, Joe, was a pioneer and a dreamer. His dream, I believe, included getting away from his family though he didn't really know that or at least wouldn't admit it if he did. Having never gone to college or been in the military, he'd lived with his parents all his life, and even when he married Jackie, she moved in there with all of them. So, he needed a break (to say nothing of what Jackie must have needed).

One part of the dream was that he could give his kids everything he didn't have and a soda fountain in the basement. His eyes lit up whenever he'd mention it, expecting we would be as excited as he was by his vision. He wanted a full set-up with stainless steel blenders and syrup pumps, nozzles that shoot out tonic and seltzer and root beer for making Black Cows, a white Formica counter and red leather-topped swivel stools to sit at. Joe loved ice cream. I think he needed the sweetness.

"What'll ya have? Sure, whatever you want. I'll make it up just the way you like it." This was Joe's idea of heaven on earth, playing soda jerk, having a ball with his kids and ice cream in the cellar.

Besides the soda fountain, there was another part of Joe's dream. It was that he would be the champion of our family and we would all rally around him in total and endless support. He was incredibly let down on that count and even early on, knew that he would be. That was the start of a lot of trouble out in the sticks between Jackie and Joe. I heard it all, being the oldest, and carried that rumble inside. In a strange way I even think the fighting came to sooth me.

"You look just like your mother, honey! The

face, the eyes, everything." I had heard that all my life until the night I stood by his open casket when a few people told me how much I reminded them of my father. I was surprised but glad that I might be taking him along with me in a way that was obvious to others, and not overly concerned that the comparison was made, for the first time, when he wasn't looking his best.

He made an impression on me, Joe did, but still, I never quite got a handle on him. He didn't seem all real. He was sort of brownish in color, short, a lot shorter than I, and egg-shaped. I was at least five inches taller but about fifty pounds lighter. With all of that difference between us, his wardrobe presented unsolvable mysteries. His shoe size was 10½ E, mine, 8½ D. They seemed to take up an inordinate amount of room in his closet. His clothes had the capacity of a magician's hat—anything could fit into them. Putting on one of his coats or shirts was an experience in the paranormal. The sleeves dangled three inches past my fingers, the shoulders slung way past where mine ended, and the shirt collars were roomy enough to accommodate a neck-brace. They'd swim on me.

Talk about swimming . . . he once loaned me a bathing suit on a family vacation. It was tantamount to being swathed in a parachute. In the ocean, the thing ballooned up around me like an island. I could barely move, and began to feel as if I was going under. Finally, slogging my way out of the water, I collapsed in the sun. An hour later the thing was still soaked.

Joe looked about the size and shape of a Boston baked-bean but in some ways he was gigantic. I couldn't figure it.

Joe made an impression. Like in the winter of 1955, when I was six and Jackie had built a sled for me. She took the back off a wooden box, nailed two-by-fours to the bottom, attached curtain rods to serve as runners, and tied a rope to the front. The creation was complete—a sled, rough, but definitely distinct and certainly more original than the commercial ones my friends had.

At that time we still lived in Medford, a short walk from West Medford Square during a time in our history when little kids could walk to town by themselves. It was a Saturday in winter, and the snow drifted to three times a six-year-old's height. Weekends were timeless affairs and the season trans-formed the neighborhood into a pallet for prints and forts and  snowmen. I played all day, never feeling the cold, and had to return home only for lunch, imprisoned by that brief interference with my freedom. The icy air, like Cape Cod water in early summer, had no power to chill or dampen the fever of adventure and fun.

By late afternoon, the sled began to disassemble. The sides broke off and the runners were bent and threatened to quit on the next trip downhill. The day was nearly over, twilight was upon us as the group began to break up toward "home-before-dark." Finally, the sled totally gave way just as the last few kids were holding out till the day's grueling finale. I said good-bye to them and sat alone for a few minutes in the middle of ice-covered Wolcott Street on what was left of my sled: a flat bottom and a front piece with a rope.

Everything was still, the sky was clear dark and the stars in bright view. In winter, the night comes so quickly, sometimes, that you don't notice it until you're in it. I sat there and breathed, biding my time before letting go of the day to head home. It wasn't easy to do. Home was the place of love's promise and also the place where the wounds of love churned. Home was the halls that echoed with voices and words I didn't want to hear. Maybe it was the same in the other kids' houses. I don't know.

My father usually worked late, especially on Saturdays. He'd normally arrive home after eleven at night. But that night, as softly and suddenly as an Indian on the hunt, he appeared. He had come for me and found me, on that side street, two blocks away from home. I was sure he had never been there before, but there he was, coming toward me, as huge as a matinee idol on the screen at the drive-in. Bent at the waist, his arms spread wide, his face broad smiling, eyebrows peaked and eyes wide with a look that spoke "SURPRISE!" I was stunned to see him. He nearly filled the panorama, standing there framed against the sky, his face outshining the full moon. "DAD!"

He was twenty-nine then, and man, did he look beautiful. He was, twice in his life, according to Jackie, asked to sign an autograph by decidedly impaired individuals who thought he was Marlon Brando. My handsome young idol knelt down and hugged me, asked if I'd had fun that day and what I was sitting on. "Yeah, I had fun" I said, still shocked by the spectacle of his company.

"Good, and what's this?" he asked, pointing to the platform I was sitting on.

"Ma made me this sled but it's broken now."

"Hmmm, that's okay, it's fine, still good enough for us," he replied.

I don't know why, but in his arms and in that instant I think I felt complete; I was filled with him, and he, or so I imagine, with me. The moment fell wordlessly into my belly, all the bits: sled, sky, night, Joe, and me, suspended in heaven. It was an experience which formed and deformed me. To feel that connection, and then its loss, left me, as the years passed, an unwilling outcast from utopia.

He moved back slowly from our embrace, keeping a soft gaze on me; half-smiling, leaning his head to the side and regarding me as if saying, "Hey, what's the surprise? I'm always here and I always will be." He gently reached for the rope and began to pull me home. I slumped dreamily on the board as it bumped down the icy street. Everything was just right and I felt welcome, safe and already home in the world—one with him and with the night. From behind I saw smoky breath rising from his mouth as he laughed and talked and sang and jogged me homeward. I saw my own breath against the dark as I vibrated along. *Funny, the things you remember.*

sled, sky, night, Joe, and me

That night, we belonged, me and Joe. It was wonderful. It was the feeling I had always wanted. I wanted it on Christmas morning and, really, every morning. But so often, as the first decade of my life passed, holidays and mornings left me waiting and hoping. This moment, though, was in no way disappointing. It was not too short or lacking in sweetness. I think it was the ice cream Joe and I truly needed. It was love, and it made me kind of crazy. The spell of everyday life was broken and I was, for a moment, free. I was, in a sense, praying in that spontaneous manner known about in Asia. I had transcended the boundaries of my skin. And I have sought to recapture that feeling, through various means, throughout my life—sometimes for almost too long.

A few years after, things slowly began changing between me and Joe. They stayed changed. I think he might have forgotten that moment on Wolcott Street. I never quite understood how all the changes between us occurred, and never quite got over that young Joe. Mighty Joe Young. And then, before I knew it, I

Joe and me

was in the night, and people were telling me how much I reminded them of him.

Some folks think he messed up with me. Some think I messed up. Everybody's got an opinion. As far as I can tell, people get stuck together in this life. Sometimes it feels like love—and there's nothing more you can say.

Lunatic Heroes

My father drove the black four-door Oldsmobile Super 88, with my mother and baby sister up front, while my head was poked out the rear window. Roadside brush whizzed past, as I searched for the amazing three-story-high milk bottles, which told me that Fairhaven, Massachusetts was close. These monster advertisements for ice cream parlors and restaurants were one of the marvels of modern America in the 1950s. There were giant milk bottles all around the country in places like Libertyville, Illinois; Spokane, Washington; in the heart of Philadelphia; in Portland, Oregon; in Memphis; and Corpus Christi. It was estimated that if filled, some of them could contain more than 60,000 gallons of milk.

My favorite of the three we'd encounter on our trip to Fairhaven was Frates Restaurant in New Bedford, probably because my father stopped there once so he could use the rest room and I got to see it close up. Since age four, I raved about these enormities, imagining that they were remnants of fairytales, containing real milk for real giants.

No fairy tales in the car though. Things were tense around my parents, especially when they were stuck close together. Though excited about the start of summer, I had mixed feelings on the first ride down to the beach in early June. It seemed to take all day even though it was only two hours with traffic. On this trip, I just stared out at the trees and weeds, waiting for the milk bottles to appear, chin resting on my arm, which lay on the window ledge, obliviously sucking on my bicep until I'd raise up pleasing purple and red hickies, which my mother noticed because she had eyes like a periscope. That started her hollering how there was something wrong with me and if I did it again she'd kill me.

*I swear I'll murder you if you keep doing that! Do you **know** what you're doing? Why do you think it turns that color? Hah? Why? Because you're sucking the blood out of yourself. You're sucking the blood from your body through the pores of your skin, that's what you're doing? Okay?*

My father kept driving and either had no opinion

on this matter (medical or otherwise) or just failed to notice the exchange. He was usually lost in his own thoughts, unless he was watching TV, and lost in somebody else's thoughts.

Now, I hadn't thought of the marks I was making in quite the way she described, so it was a revelation. But I wasn't even getting the taste of blood in my mouth, so it couldn't be too bad. And I said, "There's no blood coming out. It's still all inside me." Then, of course, she went off because I answered back, and she yelled, *It's sick, that's what it is, okay? There's something wrong with someone who does that, who sucks on themselves until they turn purple.* She just had it in her mind that it was a crime, and threatened homicide in response. She'd rather have me dead than with a hickey on my arm.

Here, my father woke from his trance, told her to calm down and said I shouldn't do it anymore. Then he doubtlessly returned to the fears and fantasies from whence he came. I started getting antsy and feeling trapped, no towering milk bottles in sight to soothe me, so naturally I asked *how much longer is it gonna take.* I must have kept that line of questioning going because in a little while, my old man started yelling that if I continued something would happen, which presumably would not be in my best interest.

Hey, that's enough. If you ask me again I'm pulling the car over.

"If I ask you what?" I said, fully aware of the answer.

When are we gonna get there!

"That's what I'm trying to find out!" I exclaimed.

Don't be a wise-guy mistah, he said, hitting the brakes.

So, there I was, caught in the back seat with two homicidal twenty-nine-year-olds up front and an eight-month-old baby sister who I still wasn't used to having around yet and who was really good for nothin' because my mother was holding her and I couldn't even get a hand over to pinch her to see what'd happen. Life just sucked and I guess that was maybe why I fastened on to my arm like a squid.

My mother and I began spending summers in Fairhaven in a beach house located behind my great aunt Rosie and uncle Pat's place on Jerusalem Road before a series of my yet-to-be-born, tag-along siblings joined us. This summer, my sister, the first one to survive after two infant deaths, was onboard and that was all well and good, but I think her arrival made things more difficult for everybody. My father came down to the beach on weekends and usually ended up transforming ordinary unhappiness into unbearable misery by suspecting my mother had been smoking and maybe drinking with her sister and friends, and that she was wearing too much make-up and tight sweaters. Every Saturday night he took it upon himself to stage some kind of scene over his suspicions. In retrospect, I think part of the problem was that he had it in his mind to get laid when he got down there, but that didn't always work out so he was often in a foul mood all the way until he left early Monday morning. He'd spend a lot of time in bed those weekends saying he was tired from work, but I think he flopped there so just in case she had a yen for something, he'd be ready. Little did he know that a smoke and a drink would have set things up nicely for him—but he never did do anything like that. He was deeply uptight.

I don't think my mother, on her best day, was ever partial to or trusted men, but if you could distract her with a good time, which was easy, she'd forget all that and be up for pretty much anything. In later years she drank plum brandy with kippers and eggs for breakfast along with me and my friends, and then chewed tobacco right after, while we all took turns spitting for distance off the deck.

Whenever my old man'd come down to Fairhaven for weekends, bumping up the general stress level, and therefore increasing my need for an outlet, I'd find ways of hickying myself by doing it on the inside of my thigh to keep it out of view. It was work getting my head down there, but worth it because it blew off a lot of steam. You have to find ways to get what you need. Some days, when the heat was really turned up between them, I couldn't help myself, and did it on the bicep without thinking and then try to blame it on the baby when my mother spied it.

The baby didn't do it! she'd yell, while jerking me around by the offending arm.

"Yes she did, I was holding her and she starting sucking on me like she does and that's what happened."

No it didn't! And so help me Jesus don't lie to me or I swear there's gonna be curtains… hospital curtains, cause I'll can**nob**alize *you.*

Now I had no idea what hospital curtains or "cannobalize" meant until years later when my therapist suggested that it was a threat to eat me, and what she actually meant to say, according to him, was *cannibalize.* When he came up with that theory, I thought he was insane but it was still disturbing. Though never technically guilty of infanticide, as far as we know, if my mother had not been so concerned about the effect on her waistline, she could well have eaten her young. So, she could kill me and eat me but I couldn't even suck on my own arm. You just want to bite yourself.

I don't really know why I was doing all that sucking, but I suspect it was a mild form of what the young sometimes do today called "cutting." Just a way to feel something, or at least something different from what I was feeling. My release valve. (This was, of course, before I discovered another use for my penis, the

31

ultimate release valve. No need to suck on my arm after that. But for a Catholic kid finding it was a mixed blessing. The penis was both a joystick and a club to bludgeon yourself with. Once you get a grip on the gearshift to hell, you just can't let go. But, here again, you figure out that you have to find your outlets where you're able to, no matter what anyone says, even God, and one way or another, you do what must be done.)

And I didn't stop at skin-sucking. I had a number of habits. Snapping my head and neck was one, picking my bellybutton until it bled was another, and I was also a busy little nail-biter, which I could get away with when my father was around because he did it too.

My mother tried everything to break me of the habit. Her first attempt was slathering my fingers with liquid pepper, which was sold in tiny vials for this very purpose. My hands got coated with the blistering solution at bedtime, so that my lips would burn if I put my fingers near them. And it worked, at first, but it didn't take me long to get past the burn and even come to enjoy the spiciness as a sort of condiment to go along with the nails. Once that connection was made, every time I tasted anything peppery, I felt compelled to bite my nails. Today, the pepper aversion method is sometimes used with incorrigible dogs to keep them from chewing the furniture, but it's frowned upon by animal rights activists as inhumane. Animals have rights now, back then we kids weren't so lucky.

Once in a while I'd totally space out on my behavior modification treatment, and there'd be frightful screams from my little attic bedroom because I'd start rubbing my eyes and practically burn out my retinas. My mother flew in the first few times it happened, usually with a cigarette going, and too much make-up on, expecting to see me gutted by a board fallen from the rickety roof, and when she found it was the pepper in my eyes she'd say, all fake-sweet and omniscient, *See, if you didn't bite your nails this wouldn't be happening, now would it?*

On subsequent summer nights, when blood-curdling screams emanated from my room she'd tell her stupid friends out there cocktailing, smoking and shifting around in mohair sweaters, *Oh, it's nothing, he has nightmares.* And when, in their anxious wisdom, they'd suggest she check on me just in case, she'd come in and say, in a maniacal, hoarse whisper, *As God is my witness, if you wake that baby I'll kill you, and before I do I'll pour that pepper in your eyes so you can die blind.*

It was kind of a bedtime story.

Once I'd acclimated myself to the pepper and she noticed that my nails were bitten as short as ever, she moved on to the next reinforcement procedure.

In the late 1950s there were early versions of what we know as Lee Press On Nails and my mother and her friends occasionally wore them. She was told somewhere along the dope line that if she attached these things to my fingers I wouldn't be able to bite through them, thereby giving my nails a chance to grow back and possibly breaking me of the habit in the bargain. She saw this idea as a creative solution, one that also pandered to her interest in the bizarre and abnormal.

But this latest method was a problem for her, because the only ones that fit me were designed for a woman's pinky fingers and there were only four of those per box of twenty nails. So she had to shape, trim, and file the others down to size in order fit my eight-year-old hands. She seemed to resent this, as if punishing me was a massive burden she had to carry. The sight of me with those things on must have been comical and gruesome, and of course she couldn't do it when my father was around because he'd throw a shit-fit thinking she was making me into some kind of freak or transvestite. So, on those summer nights when he was staying in Boston, I'd go to bed looking like Vampira from the 1950s TV show. I can't fully explain the weirdness of negotiating nightlife with those things on, and how much it worried me. First, I thought it was bizarre and creepy. Second, it seemed to indicate that on some level I must deserve it and consequently there had to be something terribly wrong with me to have to endure such a strange and humiliating process. Nothing about it seemed fair. All I was doing was biting my nails, like dad. And now this.

At times, when wearing the claws, I'd entertain myself under the covers, in the glow of a dimmed flashlight, by making evil laugh sounds, whispering weird things in a deep voice and clawing at my face and belly with my freakish fingers. I imagined it was the hand of the wicked queen in Snow White. I was the host, lead role and audience of my own *Freak-Night Theater.* It was compelling; it lit me up, unwound and unclenched me. This, I now realize, was an early version of what would come to be a centerpiece of my inner life once puberty set in . . . a process of transforming fear into consolation, converting pain into preference, making punishments work in my favor. Whatever it may have been, I think it was the start of feeling some control inside, but I knew I was doing something that definitely pleased me.

Eventually, though, I adapted once again and the method didn't end up working, because I grew to just love chewing on those nails . . . I'd chew myself to sleep even with the pepper on them and in time almost looked forward to getting them glued on, but never to getting them off—which was actual torture.

First thing in the morning, removal of the nails involved her having to apply a solvent to my cuticles with a teeny brush while I sat and waited a minute for it to take effect and then she peeled them off each finger with needle-nose pliers. I didn't like it—couldn't get around the fact that it was just the coverings being removed. I felt like my actual nails were being pulled out. I'd yelp and pretty much cry each time.

These aren't your real nails for cry-eye, she'd say, exasperated.

"But it hurts," I'd sob. "Please, mommy, stop, stop*!*"

*Stop? You stop squawking, you're gonna wake the baby. And besides, if I **don't** take them off then what are you going to do? Huh?* She later used this idea to her advantage.

I'd get through the process each time but my real nails were taking quite a beating from the gluing and un-gluing and they wound up like something you'd find at a toxic waste dump: chipped, milky looking, and chalky to the touch. As far as I was concerned they were just great when I was biting them—only short. Not anymore . . . it was the Dracula look when the nails were on, or Night of the Living Dead when they weren't. Either way I felt stigmatized, and not in the famous good way, like the crucified, risen Christ on Jerusalem Road mind you.

On top of all this, my mother frequently threatened to ground me for tempting any one of a detailed list of rules, which included policies about: lying, talking back, not eating, making noise, waking the baby, disobeying, walking hunched and not standing up straight, not flushing, leaving dirty hand prints on towels, looking stupid, acting stupid (which she referred to as "playing Mickey the dunce") causing her to "trip over" me, coming in too early or too late, and the like. When infringements were committed, she didn't remove the nails at all and would, in fact, paint them, leaving me stuck with a choice of staying in wearing the hideous (now crimson) talons, or risk going out like that to be stoned or otherwise run off Jerusalem Road by the neighbors.

Now, her methods might have made perfect sense to adults. Maybe I just tend to see everything from the victim perspective, griping and complaining all my life about nothing more than normal childrearing in the 1950s. I don't know.

The lucky turn was that I liked those fake nails so much I'd go looking for them during the day and eat them right out of the box. Soon I was up to nearly a box a day and my mother figured it was better than real nail-biting so she supplied me with them whenever I felt a craving. She'd even carry them in her purse like mints when we were out and if I began staring at my fingernails, salivating over my bicep or showing any other signs of stress, she'd reach in her bag and shake one out of the box for me. When I'd get into twitching, neck-jerking and making warped gestures and faces as I sometimes did, she'd just pop me a nail. She used them to treat a variety of signs and symptoms, the way Ritalin is today. Plus, she was occasionally tolerant when I showed signs of being peculiar. She could be nice that way.

From as early as I can remember, my mother walked around with a puss-on and had a headache whenever my father was near her. The rest of the time she was cleaning, or more accurately scrubbing, everything in sight with 20 Mule Team Borax, spraying Germicide on all surfaces and following up with layers of air-freshener. During cleaning breaks, she chitchatted nonsense with everyone, whistled, sang or screamed and generally made my life hell. I utterly loved her and lived in fear of her. She mentally harassed and physically battered me by day and then played a starring role in my nightmares.

Jackie

Being thus infatuated and terrified, it is not a stretch to guess there were grey clouds on my psychic horizon. She was difficult to figure because she was at once so beautiful and loving, and as well, bent on dominance and inclined toward punishment. When she got wound up she acted like a drug fiend who needed a fix—as if the only thing that could calm her down about her miserable, duty-bound life and disappointing marriage was forcing me to do any and everything she said, right here and right now or else. This was the most important job she had as a mother ... making me obey. My compliance was for her convenience and to make her look good to others.

When she wasn't screaming, slapping, twisting the skin on my neck, peppering, nailing me or shoving me into a bedroom, she busied herself by preparing me for the countless dangers she perceived around her. This education was shared day in and out with alarming seriousness and often at the top of her lungs. She saw this job as the second most important aspect of her mothering: preparing me for peril.

She was always warning about the deadly effects of the thunderstorm and tree combination, icicles falling off buildings and through your skull, eyes being blown out by soda-pop bottle tops, something she called "trench mouth," even summer drafts being harbingers of every malady, strangers cutting out your liver to sell on the black market, strangers in general, the absolute conviction of being struck by lightning either down from the sky or up from the ground, constipation and diarrhea (these leading to enemas or pure squeezed lemon juice respectively), germs on every surface, breaking a tooth on cellophane packages, crossing your eyes and staying that way, fish bones leading to certain death, people who smelled bad and the toxic effects of breathing around them, all toilet seats except the ones in our house, food prepared by others, and so on and so forth endlessly.

As it turns out, *she* was the most hazardous thing in my environment so, essentially, she prepared me to be cautious and concerned about what she, and only she, represented. I was a good student and took in all the lessons. I had to because I lived alone in a world she created and ruled absolutely—there seemed only two ways to go in that world, down or in. I did both.

There were times when she was loving, cuddly and verbal about her warm feelings toward me, and those moments were essential. *Come here,* she'd say, *come to mommy,* and fold me into her arms, squeezing me tight. *Do you know how much I love you? Do you know how handsome you are and how proud I am of you? Give mommy a kiss. I love you, love you, soooo, much. Do you love me? Tell mommy how much you love her.*

And I tell her and we'd lay there wrapped in an embrace for a long time. It was warm, she felt safe

and smelled of Coppertone, and Sen-Sen breath mints. Without all that as part of the equation, I could well be wearing a bib in a loony-bin right about now. I craved and treasured her protection and tenderness. I was hurt and confused when things turned, as they inevitably did, almost daily.

And to that, I never adapted.

Risking everything late one night, I sneaked into her room at the beach house, wearing the nails she had put on me earlier. I'm not sure why I did this. I was like Odysseus running the risk of waking the sleeping giant. But it was worth it to see the object of love and fear in its tranquil, vulnerable, unruffled state. So I challenged the lethal thorn-hedge of her fury, like the prince in Sleeping Beauty, crouched near the head of her bed, my eyes accommodating themselves to the darkness, very close to her face and waited, barely breathing, my heart pounding to beat the band. There, in the damp knotty pine-paneled bedroom, I smelled Elizabeth Arden hand cream, Ivory Snow laundry detergent, Alberto VO5, My Sin perfume: the scents of my mother. I formed my hands into the claw shape over her face, and held them there, widening my eyes in imitation of the Wicked Queen in Snow White and set myself in position. Seconds later, her huge eyes rolled open; I could see their electric blue even in the darkness. I didn't have a chance to move and so remained in position like a ghastly, immobilized creature on the roadway. Her eyes were neither anxious nor angry as she dreamily took one of my hands and brought it to her lips and kissed it saying, *you better be a figment of my imagination right now,* and her eyes closed as softly as they had opened. I slipped the claw out from her limp grip and went back to bed, feeling as happy and safe as I ever remember. The relationship was complex.

My mother was always an enthusiast of creativity and held a deep interest in artistic expression, which was almost entirely unrealized in her life, and that fact remained an unhealed wound for her. She was a big fan of time I spent with paint-by-numbers projects, making braided bracelets for wearing in the summer or just drawing pictures . . . the kinds of activities my father referred to as *occupations for invalids.* Both my parents had pat terms for things. My mother, for example, would label most of what my friends and I did as *savage amusement.*

I spent a lot of summertime wandering and combing the beach when I wasn't in the cabin staring at my little sister lolling around in the playpen. The nearly deserted beach was a perfect place to stagger around aimlessly and to think profound and distant thoughts. There were creatures there, mollusks, referred to as Moon Snails. Steve D'Ambrio, who was fourteen, and known as "Stevie D," said they were really called

"Lunatic Heroes." He said that was the Latin name for them, Lunatic Heroes. These snails were active only at night and just under the sand's surface. They ate by first suffocating their prey and then boring perfect holes in other sea snails, and clams, and then sucking the insides right out through the shells, which seemed weird because they were practically eating their own kind. I never actually saw the "Lunatics" in action, but I did see plenty of the remnants they left behind. Stevie D. said the

Me and Stevie D.

Moon Snails worked better than any drill because they never broke even the most delicate shells. On my beach rambles I'd often find these slightly curved, glistening, oval-shaped shells with precise holes in them and that gave me the idea.

One night, I sneaked a fresh set of ten fingernails from the supply cupboard, and delicately bored holes in the base of each nail with my Davy Crockett jack knife leather-punch feature. I carefully strung them onto a sea-worn, knotted cord I'd found on the beach and made myself a necklace with the tips of the nails set to drape across my collarbones. I didn't just use the nails as is, though. First, I chipped them up by chewing on them, then ground each one into the old wood floor to scuff them up and then thought to imprint plier's marks on them. The project felt momentous, Homeric. It felt like art. It came from my depths, and it came out very cool. Looked like something off an Egyptian Mummy. You can occasionally find people wearing shark teeth, bear claws and monkey bones as decorations, but this piece was unique.

That weekend, the instant he viewed the necklace, my father adopted an expression of angry disgust, and saw it as a sign of future trouble, an example of time wasting, certified invalid occupation and blamed my mother. She had been initially angry about the thievery, but now, confronted with my father's dissatisfaction, loved the whole idea.

My father said, *what the heck is that?*

Mom answered for me, as she had plenty to keep hidden. *He found it,* she said.

But what is it? he continued.

Mom jumped in again, *we don't know.*

Jesus, my father said and went into the dank, sea-musty bedroom because he was "tired from work."

I was heartbroken by my father's occasional disapproving attitude toward me. I wanted to be everything he expected. During those years, he and I were generally in good shape together. He referred to me as "The Blond Hammer," which, in both of our minds, was my ring name as a prizefighter and he'd announce my entrance into the house or even just into a room as if he were on a loudspeaker and boom out: *THE BLOND HAMMER! . . . HAMMER! . . . HAMMER! Ladies and Gentlemen, 45 pounds of twisted blue steel, a one-punch knockout artist . . .* and so on. I'd be ecstatic with the fame and adulation while he trailed off making crowd sounds as I shadowboxed. It was great to feel how much he celebrated me then. Of course, over time, things changed, as they must, and unfortunately went downhill on both sides of the street. It got to the point where years later he told me he loved me because I was his son, but that I just wasn't his type of guy. He was my idol, and I needed to be his type of guy. That comment has never left me. In a way, I'm still shadowboxing for him.

There was a lot of fun to be had in Fairhaven though. The kid next door, Raymond DaSilva, was my friend from the summer before my sister was born. He lived year round on the water's edge in the cottage right next to ours. I believe his family was of Portuguese heritage, and I didn't know for sure what that meant, but they seemed just like everybody else. We'd been hanging out for a few weeks when he saw the claws around my neck that first day I wore them outside. He was only inches away from me when he spotted the necklace, started gawking, and then froze, which was weird. I just stared back at him while he remained in suspended awe. Finally, he came out of it, and was so enchanted by the accessory he wanted to know everything, including where he could get one.

On the spot I started telling a story that a dead relative had given it to me, and it was a one-of-a-kind. Sorry, but. He asked what they were and I told him my relative worked in a mental hospital where a lunatic woman got her nails torn out by a deranged man with the needle-nose pliers he'd swiped from a workshop they had in there. This was the first real story I ever remember making up other than plain lies just to get out of things.

I told Ray that the madman, who shouldn't have been let loose with the others to begin with, had a habit of eating everybody's cigarette butts and the vinyl off the backs of chairs. I told Ray that my dead relative said the man had those certain kinds of compulsions and should probably have been kept away from people. (A lot of this information was gathered from my mother who had a general fascination with the bizarre, a load of eating problems herself and who took a fleeting interest in various psychiatric food syndromes, one of which was called "pica," the eating of nonnutritive substances, and that's the one that stuck with me.) I told Ray that my dead relative thought the nail-pulling incident was the strangest case he'd ever come across in all his time working in the mental hospital and he'd saved the gory relics for years until he gave them to me not long before he died last winter around Christmas.

Ray was fascinated with everything, including how the madman got all ten of them. Ray asked, "How'd he get 'em all? Was she yellin' and tryin' t'get away? Was she trying to whack him with her other hand while he was pullin' 'em out? Was anybody comin' to help her?" Now these were good questions, and I hadn't thought any of this through yet, but all the while he was touching and counting each of the nails over and over to make sure there were ten and that they were real. I felt like some kind of god when he was doing that.

I told him that the whole scene with the madman must have been pretty bad because the Lunatic Lady lived, from then on, in a comfortable, but padded room where they watched her day and night through a big unbreakable window.

I told Ray that for her own protection, she was never allowed out of that room alone, the way de-clawed cats are made to stay indoors by their owners. I told him that the even weirder part was that lots of patients and people who worked there, including my dead relative, said she was sometimes witnessed outside that padded room and that deep and long scratch marks would inexplicably turn up on people like crop circles in the night. For all her life after that she was considered mysterious, dangerous, and powerful.

Ray was hypnotized. I became a little concerned about weaving such a big lie, but it was exciting, so I kept the story going. Ray asked if they ever saw her out of her room in the daytime. I said it was in the dark, and always after midnight. He kept touching the nails, one by one—eyes locked on them, not a grain of skepticism in him.

And right then, putting together in my head the look on Ray's face when he first saw the necklace, his meek jealousy, and general straight-ahead approach, I told him that those nails had special powers. They allowed me to drill right into the minds of others and see their thoughts and also to know what animals and all of nature were about in land, sea and sky. Here, Ray was struck dumb, dizzy and bug-eyed. He actually had many such moments of absolute wonder, and they came naturally to him. He found his tongue, jumped up and down and screeched, *Show me, Show me! Show me! Read my mind!* I said the nails weren't telling me anything then and the time had to be right. We were buddies and this aspect of the summer became huge fun for the two of us. From here on, many things I knew were transmitted from the Lunatic Lady, and therefore many things Ray did were informed by her. We were sort of a cult. One founder, one follower.

Later that season, Ray ate poison ivy and almost died. I was saved because I had read the Official Boy Scout Manual (which I loved and was the first book I made to look dog-eared, thumbing through it and massaging it for hours till it looked like an heirloom Bible). The Manual informed me that in late summer, poison ivy grew berries and turned radiant colors. Ray said no it didn't—I said yes it did, and he ate it to prove his point. Chewed and swallowed three leaves at once. Soon as he did he stood and looked at me with a tooth-deficient grin then went completely blank, and stayed that way for a while. The next thing I knew he was running serpentine and silent toward his house with his hands on his head. For me, it was one of those moments you just can't fit all inside. I watched Ray run out of sight, and stared down at the disguised poison ivy plants, stunned. I trotted back home all tied in a knot and a little later saw an ambulance come to Ray's house. I was afraid he was a goner and felt responsible. I never said anything to anyone about it. I wanted to throw up.

I didn't see Ray for two days until he appeared, pressed against the big front window of his little sea-side home, opening his misshapen mouth to show me the inside of his cheeks and tongue which were swollen wide and crammed with sores. I stood outside in his sandy front yard wrapped in awe and gratitude for the Boy Scouts of America and their book. Even though his eyes were swollen, he could see that I was thrilled by the spectacle of him, and from behind the glass he was smiling as best he could, looking both delighted and somewhat Asian. I was dying to get at him, but couldn't because he wasn't allowed to leave his house yet and his folks had to feed him mushy food and keep him on medicine for a while.

That weekend, my father, not a huge fan of Ray's to begin with, saw him on his front stoop, barely recognizable, and asked me, *is that Raymond DaSilva?*

"Yes," I said.

What's wrong with him?

I said, "He ate poison ivy."

I have my answer, my father said, hands raised in

clarified surrender.

The story goes that Ray's throat closed immediately after he chomped on the plant and he was spared senseless death due to the heroic measures of the ambulance and emergency room personnel. Ray automatically believed, from that day forward, in the power of the Lunatic Lady's nails, and treated me with a kind of frightened admiration, like I was a wizard of nature. He asked me how I knew about the poison ivy and I said I just knew it and that it had just come to me. Never told him about the Manual, I guess because I wanted to keep the legend alive and the story going. Ray was dead sure it was the nails that were responsible for my insight.

All in all he was great to play with, and though on the small side, Ray was about the toughest eight-year-old in America. I was for- tunate to have practiced punching, grappling, climb- bing, and "bustin-stuff- up," with a constantly smiling, ferocious pygmy. And though fun, smart was not yet his strong suit, and now there were grave doubts if it ever would be. After the

Ray and me

incident, I had control of Ray's mind. This was a first for me.

Another interesting outcome was that Ray's parents heard from the doctor that in the future he would probably be less sensitive to poison ivy (and other poison plants), as his ordeal left him somewhat immunized. The way this news struck Ray was to put him in a trance of power. He said he believed that the Lunatic Lady, from beyond the grave, and through me, tried to stop him from eating the plant in the first place and when he didn't pay any attention, she still rewarded him for his trouble by making him poison-resistant. Ray thought he was like Superman in that way—plant poisons bouncing off him like speeding bullets. Once he was restored to health, Ray wondered if he should try it again just to see the extent of his new powers, and we decided to wait for an answer from the necklace.

It was good to know that poison doesn't always kill you and though it makes you sick, it can also make you stronger. I really liked Ray, and in a way that was new for me, felt I understood him.

Then something happened near the end of summer. Can't say too much because I don't really know. But it was one night when I heard my father snarl something at my mother and heard her shrill response. I crept over to the top of the little twisted staircase from my tiny room tucked up there in the eaves, and saw a dark blur of motion below in the den, I heard some bumping around and muffled sounds from mom. I stretched my neck through the railings and saw something. The best I can say is that I saw him try to control her. Probably was nothing, and probably things like that happened in lots of families. But still, I wanted to shout out, do something, run, fight for someone, but I couldn't. That night with my head poked through the slats, I froze just like Ray did when he ate poison ivy.

Minutes later I felt the urge to suck on myself to really see if the blood could come through my skin and into my mouth enough so I could spit it out on the floor, but my tongue was too dry so I didn't try it. Whatever happened, it must have freaked me pretty bad because I didn't bite my nails or hickey myself for a while. I began to care about my mother in a new way. And even though she never let up with me, I kept her and all of it inside . . . the habits and the hurts. It was the best I could do.

That next night after I'd watched them downstairs, I was outside with Ray following dinner. It was about dark, and we were burning tiny piles of dried grass and seaweed in my back yard. The ocean sounds and smells were constant so that you hardly noticed them, but this night they were vibrant and everything felt just the way you always want summer nights to feel no matter how old you get. The air was cozy and comforting. Ray, as usual, was seeing fireflies; whether or not they were actually there I couldn't be sure. We looked up at the constellations, checked for shooting stars and felt the gaze of the serene, orange moon overhead. There seemed to be nothing wrong and nothing but the infinite sky and the vast sea around us.

Ray and I had become blood brothers earlier in the summer, meaning that we cut our thumbs with my jack-knife and mingled our blood by pressing our slippery thumb pads together on a jetty while we sweat in the burning sun and said something about loyalty to one another for ever. Then we left crimson thumbprints and spit on a white rock which we buried in the sand and washed our wounded hands in the sea. To us it meant that we could say and do anything and we'd always be okay with whatever it was. It meant we could swear, pee any place we liked, and talk about stealing gum and licorice. It meant that between the sky and the sea, we had created a world.

We sat and burned our mini-pyres, laughed and swore. Swearing was a great source of joy for me and Ray, and it wasn't really even swearing . . . we'd say that someone was a *nutless wonder*, or a *dork, dim-wit, dick-weed, nimrod,* a *pud,* an *idjit,* a *retard* and that if so-and-so *had a brain he'd be dangerous* and *if brains were dynamite he wouldn't have enough to blow his nose* or *launch a ping-pong ball.* We talked endlessly about *nut-sacks, homos, queers* and *fags*, though we didn't really know much of what any of that meant. Mostly we learned all this from the big kids in the neighborhood, especially Stevie D., who was a source of boundless information, and who supplied us with his old knives, firecrackers, and his ideas about girls, monster movies, Elvis, and how great drinking beer would one day be.

For some reason that night, right there under the sky of great heaven, I asked Ray if he'd give me a hickey on my bicep. I told him that it had just come into my head. I told him sucking on your arm gets the blood to come right up through your skin. He said he'd do it, but he'd want me to do it to him too because we were blood brothers. I said I wouldn't, and he said neither would he then. And we agreed that since we were already blood brothers, one oath and one ritual was enough for a lifetime. That was the end. We just kept burning grass piles in the dark and stayed quiet. Staring into the flames, I considered telling him the necklace was communicating something to me, but I didn't. I learned that you have to be prepared to pacify yourself if you need to, and don't ask your friends to do it for you if you can help it. And I learned that sometimes, if you like someone enough, it was okay to quit telling the story.

I kept everything inside until that last Sunday night of August, leaving Fairhaven, on the way back home to our apartment shortly before fourth grade was to start up. It wasn't dark, but on its way, when I saw those milk bottles in the dusk of fading summer, and watched the last one disappear in my father's side-view mirror. That night, in the back seat, thinking about the beach and Ray, I touched the necklace, anticipated tomorrow, then bit and sucked all the way home and nobody knew.

Swamp

By the late 1950s, the oppression of Buddhists in Vietnam had become brutal. Meanwhile, in Lexington, I was just a boy and was concerned with other matters—like Bullfrog.

The bullfrog in the swamp near my house was humongous. He was black, long-legged and faster than imagination. I suppose we called it the swamp because it was a stagnant, scum-coated pool of water, even though it was only a bit larger than your ordinary suburban home footprint. Sparsely wooded land and rocks, big enough to climb up on, surrounded it. There was plenty of scrub vegetation and vines were hanging here and there.

It lay in the middle of the next lot over, where

one day a large house would stand. But from 1957, when I came across it, until 1963, it served as our rain forest, animal refuge, scenes for Black Lagoon Monster fantasies and the center of our wildlife experiences. In short, it was the other side of the world—sixty feet from the house. All us neighborhood kids and our dogs went there alone and in packs to see salamanders, their clear ribbons of eggs, tadpoles, garter snakes, toads, snapping turtles, and the fish we referred to as "carp." We'd go there to poke sticks, toss rocks and, especially, to meditate on Bullfrog.

He was around every spring, Bullfrog was, and all summer and a good part of each fall—and legend held that in winter, he retired to the mud on the swamp floor where he'd suspend himself under the ice cover, growing larger in silent darkness—still—impenetrable—employing the mad yogic skills that we'd heard about, until March, just after the arrival of the brave crocuses, when he'd reappear to mystify and elude us for another season.

You could never get too near him; it was as if he had a scanner somewhere on the lot. He'd leap virtually before the first sound of a footstep crackle and you'd hear the *BLURP*, followed by a parting and closing of green slime. Sometimes, if you'd been there a while, you might catch a glimpse of his eyes piercing the surface—usually you'd see his entirety only in mid-flight from the swamp's edge, fully extended for an instant before he'd slip beneath the murk—and you counted yourself fortunate to have had such a vision.

I respected him in a strange way, and was also a little afraid of him—something to do with the sensational chasm between us. He represented a tremendous mystery, and I was awed by the namelessness of what I sometimes felt. How *did* he actually live in the winter? Did he know *me* in some way—was he aware of some individual impression of me as I was of him? Did he know things—deep and distant things that only frogs but not human beings could know? This, of course, was all quite impossible to decipher because he was, essentially, inscrutable—but, at the time, it was all part of the meditation on Bullfrog in which I regularly engaged.

Though he was wholly and totally other, I felt connected to him, to say nothing of the fact that he lived next door. It was his spot—his place on the other side of the world—in what I had embraced as a part of my world. And he kept it under his quiet control and discretion, living a silent and contemplative life, shrouded in his damp and shadowy monastery.

Conversations over those summers, as we wiled away hours on the swamp banks, often went like this:

"Hey, j'ya see Bullfrog yet?"

"Naw, but almost."

"Yeah, me too."

"Danny Tuden says he touched him yesterday."

"What? He's lyin'."

"Yeah, he's lyin'."

And so on.

Catching Bullfrog was a fantasy many of us had, the way catching a troll or a unicorn may have been for some—or seeing Bigfoot, an alien or the Loch Ness Monster was for others. I don't think I truly wanted to capture him—it was, for me, a magnificent dream that I wanted to remain a dream, the kind that if you wake from is gone, never to return in the same way . . . and I wanted to dream . . . to remain in my youthful, languid summer slumber . . . and I needed Bullfrog and the swamp to lay there with me. Restful in contented lethargy.

Inevitably kids fell off the rocks and into the swamp at least a few times each summer. You couldn't really drown—unless you were like two years old and panicked, forgetting that the water was probably not *all* the way over your head (except if you landed in the very middle—and what the heck were you doing *there* anyway?). I'd seen four-year-olds extricate themselves from their impending watery graves through sheer determination and the power of their blood-curdling screams. And we'd always extend a stick or a belt to a little kid if he was standing there chest deep, coated with green scum and draped with salamander eggs, stuck in the mud, shaking and hollering that some unspecified entity had hold of his leg or something.

Those immersions were badges of merit and holy rites of passage—and you'd hear kids say, even years later, "I fell in once . . . it was weird." The swamp was a sort of turned-around Fountain of Youth. Once you went into it, you aged . . . or at least your soul got older. Perhaps it was a kind of baptism by fire reserved for us by Brother Bullfrog.

One time, years later, Penny Rousseau fell through some of the snow-covered rocks that surrounded the swamp on a late December afternoon as the sky was darkening during a windless and heavy snowfall. I was in my driveway and thought I heard muffled cries beyond the snow banks that framed our yard. As I approached the swamp I saw the tips of trembling, frost-covered fingers poking up through the frozen crust in a gap between two huge rocks. Being much older than she was, I was able to pull her straight up and out by her wrists. She emerged, unexpectedly coatless, with her eyes popping out of her head, and the moment her toes hit the ground she spun wordlessly and dashed across the street to her house, disappearing into the hush of thick snowflakes crying, "Help, help, Mommy—HELP! I'm sorry!"

These hysterics were in no small measure due to the fact that her mother was a colossal tyrant, a squint-eyed stick of a woman, who was known in the neighborhood for the thrice-daily ringing of a large, hand-held, brass bell used to summon her nervous, Pavlovian offspring home. And God forbid if the dog got there before those kids did—we could only imagine the hell there was to pay.

Mrs. Rouseau was known over the years for yelling at her children and husband, other neighbors, and each of us kids at one time or another for various infractions and infringements of which we had been entirely unaware prior to the ferocious, bell-ringing-accompanied reprimands we'd receive. It was an effective and disorienting method, I'll tell you, and we could only stand there dumb and deafened during the ceremonial and clamorous chastisement. My mother referred to her as "That lady with that friggin' bell."

Evidently, Penny, while trapped in the crevice, had been hearing the bell's repeated and increasingly vigorous ringing, and it being the first time in her nine years she hadn't run full-tilt to her house, she must have assumed that she was dying, or dead, trapped there in some kind of gothic nightmare, thirty yards from her front door. Mrs. Rousseau might have heard her daughter's plaintive cries if she'd only laid off clanging that infernal thing.

I didn't see Penny around again till spring when I witnessed her mother demonstrating bell-ringing techniques to her on the front steps so she could qualify to summon her brother, Gary (often known to be at large himself and who accounted for most of the neighborhood cacophony). I believe the ordeal had proven too much for Penny and she'd taken to becoming a siren instead of an explorer—giving up her dream of a brave and adventurous life—putting it off for a while, or perhaps forever.

Swamp experiences had a way of changing you.

One summer afternoon some big kids I didn't know—there were three of them—were at the swamp when I arrived, and they had just caught Bullfrog. To me it was as if they had discovered Atlantis. I clicked into overdrive.

"Hey, that's the frog," I said, astonished and practically disoriented.

"No shit, Sherlock," one of the boys answered.

"Wow, can I see him?"

"You got eyes, you can see him."

He was not so dark after all, but a deep and vibrant green. With large teenage hands around his belly, he had stretched himself right out, and man, if he wasn't eighteen inches long. I was already hypnotized when the boys began walking away from the swamp with him towards my house, which was odd to me because I didn't know them and doubted they even knew it was my yard they were walking into. I wondered why they'd be taking him anywhere. I couldn't fit the entire scene in my head . . . Bullfrog, coming over to my place . . .

visiting his neighbor, kind of.

"*Wa-Watcha doing?*" I asked, eager but somewhat agitated to be a part of this momentous and auspicious occasion.

"Just watch," one of them said authoritatively.

They set Bullfrog down at the bottom edge of my front yard and when I saw him there, out of his place and against the green of the grass, he seemed to change. Darker again, like in the water, but now smaller and stone-still, never attempting a getaway, not the slightest effort to spring into flight as was his typical course of action. Perhaps, I imagined, he was employing his wintertime competencies—his yogic trance—remaining in deep reserve. Perhaps it was something else that kept him there . . . maybe some of that deep and distant knowledge I suspected he possessed, or possibly the same thing that held me there as the boys hurriedly fumbled with their pockets. I could barely wrench my eyes from him and only briefly glanced in the direction of the three others. Before I knew what was happening, one of them had forced open Bullfrog's mouth and jammed in a firecracker. Bullfrog remained ever motionless—accepting—apparently peaceful. He might have been in shock—but he just stood there in a wide stance, looking stable and strong.

Now, I was gripped with anxiety. My legs shook. I felt woozy, but I knew I had to act.

"*Hey,*" I started to move forward.

"Hey what?"

"*What are ya gonna do?*" I asked, stopped in my tracks.

"Whaddya think, jerk-off?"

"*No, don't,*" I croaked.

"Who is this fucking kid?" one of the others asked.

"Never mind him," his friend said as they bent to their task.

"*Hey, wait,*" I blurted out impotently.

"Shut up," one shouted. . .

And I did.

And the match was lit and put to the wick. I didn't fly to pull it out, didn't yell for my mother, didn't shout for help, didn't fight for what I knew was right. I didn't do anything. I stood by, mute, frozen, afraid, stupid.

And it went off.

Bullfrog's head jerked up and then came back with stunning speed. His mouth blew wide open, but he remained still—his eyes fixed straight ahead. I didn't know if he was dead, standing there. I didn't know what was happening to him . . . or me. The sound of the blast was deafening—Bullfrog's mouth remained hanging open. The aftershock and shrieking and hoo-hahs of the boys started coming in and hurt my head. I felt the sounds all through me now, and thought I was going to fall right down there, or throw up, and I raced back to the swamp—dissociated, smashing blind through the brambles. I hid by the rocks on the other side of the swamp choking back my shame and rage-filled tears. Lying down on a low rock, holding my head, I saw my face reflected in the water darkly. Time passed, but to me it just hung there—not moving, not stopped, as I wildly thought about what I should have done.

When I returned to my yard there was no sign of the big kids or of Bullfrog. I frantically searched the spot on the grass and saw shreds of paper and a tiny impression where the detonation had occurred. I stumbled around confused, and queasy. I had no idea what to do or where they went—I wanted to believe that he was okay, and had taken off, hiding himself in the bushes waiting for his time to go home, but I felt a sinking and certain knowledge they had carried his shocked and injured body away to do it again somewhere else in order to finalize the deed—to get what they wanted from him—his suffering and his life. If he wasn't dead yet, I knew that soon he would be, and I also knew that I had been awakened and that the dream was over. No more youth, no more summer sleep—the bell had been rung for me now, but this one did not call me home, and soon I would have no choice but to climb through the ropes and into the war.

I was too ashamed to tell anyone—afraid they'd ask what I did and why I didn't. My head hung down inside me after that, near a heart which leaked and burned. I hid. I hid because I let them . . . I let them wake me . . . let them take me. I handed myself over to them, and so I hid. And now, a half century later, I carry his weight and meditate on him still. His sacrifice and my lack of strength contributed to my fantasy of becoming an avenging angel—protecting the helpless, coming to the rescue of the disenfranchised, standing up against abuses of power. I tried to do these things, but not frequently and seldom well. In fact, most often, I've had regrets about the parts I played—overreacting unnecessarily and inappropriately or, when real action was called for, freezing. Never enough, not nearly enough, to rinse the guilt from my hands.

Five years after Bullfrog's passing, a Buddhist monk self-immolated in South East Asia on June 11, 1963, in a protest against the brutal oppression by the Catholic regime in power in Vietnam. The monk had prepared for months in meditation and, at a busy intersection, his fellow monks poured gasoline on him and then he lit the match. It was an act of tremendous courage and a sign to the world that he and his brothers could withstand any pain for the sake of his people. It was the most powerful image I had ever seen and it brought back the stalwart and resolute figure of Bullfrog standing firm in the face of his oppressors and it also recalled my passivity in the face of his courage.

The *New York Times* reporter who was present at the Vietnam burning wrote:

> *"I was to see that sight again, but once was enough. Flames were coming from a human being; his body was withering and shriveling up, his head blackening and charring. In the air was the smell of burning flesh; human beings burn surprisingly quickly. Behind me I could hear the sobbing of the Vietnamese who were now gathering. I was too shocked to cry, too confused to take notes or ask questions, too bewildered to even think . . . As he burned he never moved a muscle, never uttered a sound, his outward composure in sharp contrast to the wailing people around him."*

The story goes that, even after the incident, though he was cremated in Buddhist tradition, his heart would still not burn, and is therefore considered holy and has since been in the custody of the Reserve Bank of Vietnam.

This was the strength and power Bullfrog demonstrated to me in my boyhood; the passion and empathy evoked in me by him and the monk was unforgettable, immeasurable, bottomless. The monk who gave his life was a hero to me, as was Bullfrog before him.

And so the swamp was irrevocably transformed

for me on that, my tenth summer, but I continued to visit, sitting on the rocks at its edge for years after, staring at the water, seeing my changing face reflected back, as I did on that day when I first saw my shame and sorrow in the swamp's mirror.

In speaking with my brother about those days he said, "Y'know, a lot of the swamp still existed even after the McAllisters built their house on that lot—more than half the swamp was still out in their backyard. Then they built their swimming pool and that killed the rest of it." A moment later he said, "Hey, I wonder where it is, the swamp? Gotta be under there somewhere, no?"

"Yeah," I replied, "gotta be."

I did not mention that, although the swamp itself is gone, I keep it with me, my piece of the other side of the world. Perhaps I hang on to it in the hope that it will prevent my heart from burning up. And I have maintained my position on the rocks. The picture in the water continues to be my dark reflections, of which I seem tireless. But since that summer, in the swamp swims an image of Bullfrog which, from time to time extends into full-view, breaking the still surface, disturbing the static reflection—contorting and twisting it until it becomes more real, more me.

IN MEMORIAM

Bullfrog (Summer, 1958) / Thich Quang Duc (Summer, 1963)

Meat

I was ten years old in the sixth grade at the Lincoln School in Lexington, Mass., a good year younger than the other kids. It was my first time in the public education system. Up until then I had attended Mrs. Casey's Bartlett School which was situated in a stately old home on a quiet side street in Arlington.

Mrs. Casey, the principal, lived on the third floor and her daughter, Noreen, was one of the teachers. So was Miss Karr, who was beautiful. I used to get a funny sensation in my belly when I watched her write on the blackboard with a new piece of chalk. Miss Karr employed the Palmer method of penmanship. This style of writing involved muscle motion, in which the muscles of the arm were used for movement, rather than the fingers. And something about that quite interested me.

My sexual ideas had not been fully formed, but there was something waiting inside. My course in these matters took lots of twists and turns, just the way the Palmer method did.

Mrs. Casey's was a very small school where only ten to fifteen children comprised each class from kindergarten through the fifth grade. The reason I found myself in public school was because we moved from the second story apartment my parents rented in Medford out to Lexington and into our own home. This was a pretty big deal, but not as exciting for me as it was for my parents who believed they had just achieved the American dream, though by then the marriage was already at least half-trashed. Still, they hoped to make it all come true somehow and this move to "the sticks" was a high point for them in that eventually futile effort. For me, though, torn from my cozy school, my neighborhood friends all gone . . . I was lost. Small. Young. Lost.

I was lost in a school building that was so vast it frightened me to roam in it unsupervised. (When "The Shining" came out twenty-two years later it brought me right back to the massive, dark halls of the Lincoln School.) A lone walk down a corridor to an administration office nearly overwhelmed me. I was never a brave child. I was not sheltered; I just lived with an abundance of available fear.

On a warm September morning, a boy about thirteen, who already appeared to have the rudiments of a beard, walked up to me in the roomy school entrance and asked me if I had ever *beat my meat* in the bathtub. I had had no formal orientation to the school and I believed his question was designed as a welcome and an invitation to friendship. Having never heard that particular expression, I relied on his miming of the activity to discern what he meant. He'd made a fist with his right hand and, with the outside edge of it, made an up and down motion toward and away from his crotch in a rapid rhythm . . . like punching. I told him that I hadn't ever done that and he strenuously recommended it saying, "You gotta try it . . . it's unbelievable in the tub." (Of course today, a kid making sexual gestures to a new ten-year-old student would be reported to the authorities and placed on a sexual offenders list for minors. His parents would be investigated by the DSS on suspicions of abusing him and he would be in a chemical restraint, in therapy and enrolled in a new school for deviants.)

I was caught by his suggestion. Mind you, I was the child of Catholics, it was the late 1950s and I, along with most of the country, lived a short distance from my body, to say nothing of the fact that I was a long distance from puberty. My sexual development was, to say the least, delayed. I was such a late bloomer, in fact, that when my father decided to speak to me about sexual matters at age thirteen, he thought he'd quiz me first to find out what I might already know on the subject. I told him that I thought the boy put his *"peeshy"* (now imagine at age thirteen, I was still referring to the penis as a *peeshy*) into the girl's lower back. This notion had come to me from watching dogs in the neighborhood getting busy with one another twenty years before leash laws had been instituted.

There was a considerable amount of *badonk-a-donk* going on within the pet population back then since, like kids, dogs were free to roam. And it seems that steaming piles of poop everywhere and public displays of animal carnality did not offend the sensibilities of the human population enough for them to do anything about it. Dogs seemed a lot better then. So did kids (not me, but other kids). Dogs and kids were more street-smart, more confident, more fit, more happy, and as it turns out, more horny. But, as rambunctious as dogs were, they didn't have hands, and therefore could not beat their meats. In general, it seems that once a species develops hands, a lot of trouble starts in the devil's workshop.

(*As an aside: the ancient Greeks had no word for what we call hands. The word they used actually included ten inches of forearm. Dogs have forearms and so, at least by ancient Greek standards, dogs have hands and could, technically, beat their meats. But, as we all know, they choose not to, and we profess envy of them for their relaxed capacity to lick their meats. I've drifted here, I know.)*

Well, the very night the suggestion was made to me by my nearly-bearded, self-appointed sexual mentor at the Lincoln school, I sat in the tub at home and began the now clearly ludicrous process of pounding myself in my groin. This activity caused bathwater to splash wildly all over the place. I was getting it in my eyes and choking on it too, since, while gasping with shock and pain, I inhaled it from time to time as it flew up and out of the tub. Water was rolling on the bathroom floor, and I would have been too had I not been confined by the walls of the tub while I sprawled there groaning and punching myself in the nuts. It was a painful and entirely unfulfilling experiment but I was dedicated to the idea that there must be something in it for me and so I carried on, banging away like some demented, craze-fisted sea monkey.

The next time I saw the kid he asked me had I done it yet.

"Yeah," I said.

And he asked, "So, how was it?"

"Great!" I replied.

"I told you," he said, beaming and brandishing his jiggling fist.

Even though it wasn't true, I persisted on that course of action, or gentler variations of it, until one day, it all began to make sense. And the devil's tools and workshop converted into a fortress of dark joy.

And so, there at the Lincoln School, I began my making up stories about sexual activity. Not yet a month in the public education system, and already the purity of that new piece of bright, white chalk had been jerked right out of Miss Karr's hand. But in the bargain, I had discovered the power and protection of telling tales.

And, as it so often turns out, one man's meat is another man's story.

Nonno

I clutched the brown paper bag to my ribs as I walked, slowly and deliberately, five paces in front of the man in the fedora and long camel coat. He had a pistol trained on me from inside his pocket, the barrel pushing the pocket pointedly towards my rigid back as I tread the forty yards to the Shawmut Bank.

The thousands of dollars in the package were my responsibility and I was breathtakingly aware that if anyone so much as bumped into me I risked being shot, perhaps repeatedly.

My grandfather (whom I referred to as Nonno) was "old school" and felt that rather than carrying the deposit from our family business to the bank himself, compelling me to do so was the safest and smartest way to go. So, he regularly aimed a fully loaded, partially rusted, probably never fired, and certainly never registered, nickel-plated, .38 caliber revolver at me to insure that the money made it down the street to the teller's window, at which point he took over the banking transactions.

Never mind that, at mid-day in the summer on busy Salem Street in Boston's North End, an eleven-year-old boy would be carrying a stash of thousands in a paper bag is so far-fetched that it could easily have served as deep cover, averting any ne'er-do-wells poised on the corner behind Polcari's lemon slush stand. This was not enough for Nonno. He had to make it obvious that something was up by shadowing me with a firearm. It was as if, in 1960, when the scene actually took place, time stopped for that short walk and the two of us were cast in a fantastic movie, set in the depression era.

Boston's North End

His classic clothing, the street and air thick with the smear and scent of foods and spices and sounds, along with our purposeful, tandem gait seemed to continue on in slow motion as if we were serene and rendered in sepia tones while the rest of the neighborhood rushed around in the high-speed Technicolor heat. I remember people looking at us, a large man wearing a long coat in the summer swelter, and a robotic little kid with a determined expression and cyclopean focus. I never averted my gaze from the bank, which was in plain view for our entire journey, under strict admonition from my grandfather to: "No look at nobody, no talk to nobody, walk straight and no even look at Nonno." I took my job seriously, and I trusted in his reconnaissance abilities. I was sure to foil any of the many crooks I was persuaded lurked and lingered about.

My father tried, to no avail, to convince him not to trail me with the gun. My father told me that Nonno didn't know anything about guns and that he might go off in fits and start shooting uncontrollably at the least provocation. He told me that there was actually no danger in the street save for that supplied by Nonno himself. He told me not to do what Nonno said. He told me that his father was stupid and crazy.

I didn't give a rubber cannoli about anything my father said about it. That short journey to the bank represented the pinnacle of my achievement and worth.

I was no way giving up my role as secret agent and stealth deflector responsible for the lifeblood and financial safety of my entire family. Plus I got to be a full-fledged collaborator with a gun-toting maniac.

This was really living. This was cool.

We were cool. We were the most dangerous and important figures on that tiny side street. We thought we were better, tougher and smarter than Al Capone and Bugs Moran even if to some we might have been more like Captain Kangaroo and Howdy Doody.

The maniac was my biggest fan and I his.

Nonno was different from most of the others in our family—from his twin sons and his wife—not so much from his two daughters who, like him, were expansive and impractical and fun loving. But, they were the product of his first marriage. He had been in the U.S. since age sixteen, fighting to make a living, and got married in his early twenties, when his wife of seven years died of pneumonia, and left him with two little girls. Desperate, he called the small town in Italy which he had left a decade earlier for help from his family, but somehow, right in Boston, he met a girl from the very town he'd left and who had the same last name as his.

Of course it did not seem odd to me that my grandparents had the same last name, nor that all the members of her family, my great aunts, and uncles, all of them had the same last name as I did. When I was old enough to ask how that could be, my father and his brother swore to high heaven there was no blood relation between them. But when you think of it, the town had fewer than 300 people around that time, and she appeared, a mere teenager, within weeks of his call. She married him after a short courtship, and took over his home and the raising of his girls. Had to be at least a cousin, no? But God help anyone who tried to make sense of it. My father, especially, would become delirious with rage at the idea.

Though Nonno was in dire straits when he met my grandmother, I know he loved her. Still, she and the twin sons to whom she gave birth ended up in inverse proportion to my grandfather's aesthetic and sensibility. For me, that turned out to be a first-rate situation.

He loved having fun. He drank wine where no one else in the family did, he overate, I'd seen him with a cigarette on an occasion, and a cigar now and then (smoking was positively abhorred by my grandmother and her sons), he played the harmonica and something else he called a Jew's harp, which had a flexible metal piece you could twang in the chamber of your mouth. He also played castanets and tambourines and practical jokes. He carried a spring-loaded knife called a stiletto to use for peeling and slicing fruit and other odd jobs requiring a blade. He had a dog for a while that he named Primo Carnera who he said was "part boxer and part wrestler." Nonno walked with a stick years before he actually needed one. I remember my father being repelled by that affectation, but Nonno was great with the thing. He whacked objects and even individuals with it frequently. He was an expert at, as the Brits say, putting a bit of stick around.

He was five feet ten inches, 325 pounds and wore all that enormity surprisingly well. Smooth, beautiful skin, face like a moon, bellybutton the dimension of a silver dollar. Wore size eleven, triple E width shoes—the shoes lined up in his closet like a string of deflated footballs. He loved clothes, an interest thought frivolous, narcissistic and a waste of resources by those twin boys of his and their mother. He wore cologne and a diamond ring; habits, my father regularly seethed, only men like Liberace had.

Nonno loved to pamper himself and those around him—those who'd let him, anyway. He was grand and lived in a grand style. He once returned from a visit to Europe with, among other gifts, five gold Rolex watches: one for himself, one for each of his sons and two for valued associates. He was known to show up at friends' homes carrying a stalk with 200 bananas on it. They'd say, "Tony, what are we going to do with all these bananas?" He'd reply, "You'll use 'em. We'll have some now," and then eat an entire "hand," which could consist of up to ten of the fruit, all the while laughing, drinking wine, telling stories and lovely, picturesque lies. He cried liberally and shouted often. More than anything, though, he laughed.

Save for his daughters, in our family, he was alone with this extravagant, ornate personality; my father, uncle and grandmother were serious nose-to-grindstone, shoulder-to-wheel people.

He didn't care about working hard himself anymore, he was interested in having others do that for him. So a lot of the time he'd spend Saturdays carrying me around Boston's North End on his shoulders, promising to buy me whatever I wanted, but almost always bought me exactly what he wanted. He'd get me an ice cream cone and then borrow it with his huge, soft hands, the fingers like Italian sausages, put it to his lips and with one bite the entire scoop was off the top. Or he'd ask for a sip of a frappe he'd just got me and drink the entire thing down so quickly he'd stagger around holding his head, groaning and laughing with brain-freeze. It was fine with me. He was unstoppable anyway—just had to do it, and I knew that—always bought you another or gave you a five or even a ten dollar bill for your trouble, and you always came out ahead.

He once collected me, my great aunts (his sisters-in-law), and other assorted friends and walked us nearly a quarter-mile to Mother Anna's Restaurant, all the way there extolling the menu and telling us that we could order whatever we wanted. It was a rare treat for my family to go out for a meal as it was considered a waste of money, and an odd idea anyway to eat food from an establishment instead of one's own kitchen or the kitchen of another family member or close friend. This belief was held by all except, of course, Nonno, who loved to eat and did it anywhere and everywhere he could. When we arrived, the waitress addressed him with respect and warmth, and he announced to her, "*Manicotti a tutti*," (manicotti for everyone) and that was the end of that, as our unopened menus were immediately cleared from the table.

It was always thought best by the adults to walk places with him because he was the worst driver anyone knew. It's not clear to me if he even had a license. I know he couldn't read in either of the languages he spoke and I think that's a requirement to take to the roads legally. When I got my driver's permit at sixteen, he gave me his only motor vehicle advice: "Stay on the right, and blow the horn." Hearing him tooting his own horn was an experience passengers and other motorists were treated to at roughly three-to-four-minute intervals, honking his way down the street, often for no apparent reason. I once asked him why he did it and he said, "Because it's good."

I don't want to give the wrong impression. He might not have been able to read, but he could definitely count and it was difficult to get anything over on him. He knew what time it was too, and *right now* was the time. He was the only one who ever gave me the idea that you could have fun in life, do it with style, and be your own man. Not just one who carries a bag of obligations and responsibilities, not just one who toes the family line, the dogma of the church, the image of being hardworking and living beyond reproach, not just one who keeps up with the neighbors. No, he was his own man—he owned himself.

By the time I was able to take full advantage of all he had to offer, he was old and ill, tolerated by his sons and cared for by those of his generation, those awaiting their turns in the final bed. His power and friends were mostly gone, the girl from that little town in Italy, long gone. The curtain had begun to descend on the stage upon which he strode so regally. But, when I was a kid, he got in on me and there he remains.

I knew he was going. Somehow, I knew. Maybe I didn't want to know. Because:

Subtract Nonno from the world—the world he knew and lived by heart—and I was left to be guided and companioned by minor players.

Subtract Nonno from the world and you have a smaller, emptier place where the sun sinks a little lower and the roads of the world grow darker.

Subtract Nonno from the world and I'd be left

without the glowing wine of his company and the warm smile of his lunar face.

He strode across the proscenium and I was a player in the show. I shared the stage and stood beside him, and sometimes in front of him, in the spotlight, which he trained on me like that revolver. Never in his shadow, always held up on his massive shoulders to feel the light. It was the way he loved me.

My grandmother, Cousin Frank, Nonno, me, Jackie,
Cousin Tony

Nearly half a century has passed since those days in the North End, and more than thirty years since Nonno took his last halting walk. I'm still carrying the lifeblood of my family, but I have given away so many things. Some have been taken and some have been lost. There have been times since where I felt I'd reached the edge of the earth and that I might fall from the world's end and into the void of despair.   But I did not . . . perhaps because I've kept some of *him* with me.

I miss him, and would be delighted to stand, once more, in front of a loaded gun for a final walk together.

Bully

I was appalled and saddened by the events in South Hadley, Massachusetts in 2010. Fifteen-year-old Phoebe Prince had been so tormented by a group of girls that she eventually hanged herself in the school clothes she'd been wearing on the last day in hell, unable to bear that cross any longer. She chose no life at all over the one she was living. Her body was found hanging at home, in a stairwell, by her twelve-year-old sister. Phoebe's family had been to the school a number of times to complain, to no avail. On the final day, the group of girls followed Phoebe, verbally abusing and threatening her in the school hallways as they had been for months, as well as in the library, classrooms, lunchroom and bathrooms, and finally, once again, on the street, on the way home, calling her "Irish Slut" and

"Irish Whore" while pelting her with open soda cans from a passing car. The scene is ferociously cruel.

Her family, in this country for less than a year, went through the appropriate channels at the school, and for their efforts they got a box with their child inside. Many vicious comments were posted on the Facebook memorial page her family set up following her death and it had to be taken down.

They decided to bury her in Ireland, wanting, I imagine, to surround her in soil which still had some heart left in it.

There have always been people who threaten and bully others, and if you think about it, you realize they will always be with us. And, if you look closely, you see that sometimes, we are they.

Phoebe Prince did not have the benefit of my father. Neither did her tormentors.

I got pushed around, and terribly frightened by a giant in the sixth grade. I was ten years old, a year younger than the other kids in my class at the Lincoln School. The giant was called Stossel. (I don't know if that was his last name, or if he was called that because it sounded big, like "Colossal.") He was thirteen and was reported to be six feet tall and 200 pounds. He had a stack of blond hair atop his mammoth head and a vast chest. To me, he was a walking Alp.

Stossel himself was probably a good kid who had

been warped by hormones gone wrong, then emotionally twisted from the burden of being viewed as a freak by both children and adults. He was likely full of rage, and so took it out on the most vulnerable of his peers. I was the smallest in the class as well as the youngest, and to see us side by side must have created a fairy tale picture of giant and dwarf.

This Colossus, this thirteen-year-old mountain (who was also considered to be a mental midget for being thirteen in the sixth grade), beat me like a drum one Friday afternoon, and dragged me through the woods, to the Old Reservoir, where I thought for sure he'd kill me and leave my body floating for the police and my parents to find on Saturday morning. I survived the ordeal, but waited fretfully till Sunday night, after Disney, before telling my parents what had happened to bring me home so dirty and skittish on Friday afternoon. I only brought it up then because I was scared to go back to school the next day.

Had the mauling I endured occurred today, it would have eventually involved a committee, therapists, and conferences between concerned parents, teachers, lawyers and law enforcement officials. It would have included medications and diagnoses for the involved parties, as well as neighborhood conversation spanning the remainder of the school year.

That Sunday night, twitching in my pajamas, I

told my father how Stossel had manhandled me; my mother was listening from the kitchen where she was making popcorn and hot chocolate. The specifics were that he got me into the woods behind the school and dragged me around by the collar of my jacket towards the Old Res, and when I tried to escape or fight back, he'd punch me in the head with the same hand he was using to drag me. This should give you some idea of how strong he was, and how utterly grim the situation was for me.

As my tale unfolded, I could see that my father was getting more and more disturbed, because when he was in such a mood he'd fold his tongue in half and bite it so the thick center of it was protruding between his teeth. As he listened, tongue on display, he nodded his head in sympathetic understanding.

My parents were both upset, and when I finished, my father paused for a second, released his tongue and said, **"GET A BAT!** J'a hear me? **GET A BAT!"**

"JOE-*OH*," my mother squealed in disbelief from behind the stovetop.

"*Never mind*," he snapped at her, then turned back to me and said, "Take a bat to school tomorrow and hide it in the yard, then later you stand near a corner of the building and call him over. When he comes around the corner, swing the bat as hard as you can right for his head. You understand me?"

I stood frozen in the face of this prescription.

"JOE-*OH*," my mother shrieked, "I could croak that kid myself, but you can't tell Sonny to do that. What are you crazy?"

"Never mind crazy. What? You want to fight his battles for him? You want him to be a mark all his life? He's *gotta* do it!"

At this point, I was shaken by everything: the experience of Friday afternoon itself still reverberating in my mind, having to tell my parents, the argument it was causing between them; but mostly, I was rocked by the anxiety, fear and thrill of getting revenge on Stossel. Even with my pajamas clinging cold against my damp flesh, I knew, in the very moment of my father's proclamation, that I would do it. I knew that with my father's guidance and permission, I was like my hero, Bond, James Bond. I had a license to kill.

My father and I went to the garage to choose the weapon. Within minutes my mother was totally on board with the plan. How could I lose? Clearly, I had been raised by wolves and here was one of the great benefits of being in the pack. My father determined that the best tool for the job was one which he referred to as a "fungo" bat. He said it would be easier for me to handle and would do just as much damage. He reviewed the plan with me a number of times before bed, quizzing me on exactly what to do when the deal went down.

I was to get to school a few minutes early and hide the bat at the rear corner of the building facing the huge schoolyard. At recess I was to spot Stossel and call him over to me while peering around the corner with the bat behind my back. When he rounded the building I was to have it cocked to unload at his face, which I wondered if I could even reach. My father assured me that landing on his collarbone or neck would be good enough. He made me swing with an upward arc a number of times gauging the relative height of Stossel's head with the ideal impact point being at the end of the bat.

I didn't sleep much that night.

In the morning the plan was activated. After an especially hearty breakfast, which I only dabbled with, and an anxious look from my mother while she touched my cheek, my father drove me to school. On the way there, he squeezed the top of my head a couple of times and said, "Don't worry." Once we got there, he looked me in the eye and said, "Get him," like he was talking to a Doberman. I left the car, books and bat in hand, and my father watched till I disappeared around the building where I'd planned to hide Exhibit A.

I was a distracted, mumbling hunchback for the morning classes. Not that this was so unusual for me, but today I had been conversing with more than the typical demons. My insides were churning with anxious fear. I was no longer thrilled with the prospect of revenge, nor was I as convinced that dad's sanction to carry out the act would be as indemnifying as a 007 license to kill. Faced with the actual mission, I did not feel like James Bond. No lucky number 7. At this point I only felt like the double zero. I felt alone, inept and afraid. Afraid to do it and afraid to tell my father I didn't.

The school day was a nervous blur until lunch, the thought of which made me gag. Then, recess. What had been a welcome break from the miserable drudgery of school had, on this day, become a zombie trek toward the killing fields. Whose head would roll, I did not know. But I knew something was about to change.

I walked, with my feet in a syrup of fear, to the corner of the school where the bat was hidden, and when I saw it was still there I felt nauseous. Facing the wall, I took hold of it and stood there out of view of the playground for a few minutes. Then, with the weapon in my right hand, I grabbed the corner of the building with my left and peered around until I located Stossel with his pint-sized entourage revolving around him. Somehow, I rescued courage from the jaws of terror and shouted his name. He heard me and spun his watermelon-sized head in my direction. Seeing me, he stood still, with a look on his face which said, "This midget is shouting at me with an attitude?"

Knowing I was in the battle now, I yelled, "Come 'ere!"

I saw him run in my direction like a mountain with oak trees for legs. I only had a few seconds, and disappeared behind the building, but before I was completely ready, he came skidding around it. I swung up at his head in a mighty arc, as instructed, but never quite got my left hand securely on the bat handle. Nonetheless, it was a fierce threat of a swath I cut. Stossel reared back, raised his arms to shield himself and somehow saved his face with his massive forearms, just as I turned to run like a lamb from a lion. I zigged and zagged until I was around the building at the front entrance of the school. There wasn't a sign of Stossel behind me. My heart was pounding to beat the band. I could feel the blood flowing in my eyes and hear it thudding in my ears. I didn't know what would happen next, but I knew that I had done it. I had swung the bat at his head. Whatever was going to happen would happen. I also knew my father had my back, and with that I could bear anything.

I ran into the school building and hung around the administration office until recess ended. When Stossel saw me in the hall later he said, "You're dead, asshole." One of his miniature friends said, "Yeah." I looked at them mute, worried, and witless, and stayed near teachers all the rest of the day, until my ride came to take me home.

My mother was in the kitchen when I arrived,

happy that I was uninjured and undrowned. She was also happy that she hadn't gotten a call from the school about a murder. She asked me what happened and I told her that I had done it. She was radiant with pride. My mother, bless her, she was one tough dame. I was exhausted and quiet until my father came home and when he heard the story said, "Good. Atta boy." I was afraid to go to school the next day but my father assured me, "He's not going to do anything. If he was, he'd a gotten you right away. He knows you could get him eventually with that bat. Watch what I tell you."

I was totally unpersuaded. My father didn't know Stossel, he didn't know how vulnerable I was, how afraid. He didn't know my little life really. But, as it turned out, he knew the world, and he knew that kid would never touch me again.

Stossel was too proud to go to the teachers or tell his parents that some little kid tried to smash his face in, and stupid as he was, he was too smart to mess with a maniac. I only had a couple more months at the Lincoln School before I transferred to St. Sebastian's Country Day School in Newton for the seventh grade. The entire lesson didn't take at that time, but I learned something about life and bullies after that day. I learned you have to stand up.

Had Phoebe Prince been my sister, my father would have equipped her with a small canister of pepper spray. He would have had her go to school and find a good moment to spray one of the girls in the face who had been tormenting her, kick her once in the stomach, while she lay on the ground screaming about her burning eyes, then leave the scene calmly and quietly. She would be told to keep the weapon at hand in case the girl, or any of her posse, were stupid enough to try something funny again. Had they, she would have been instructed to repeat the scenario with each of her tormentors. Phoebe would have felt empowered. She would have been respected, or at least feared. She would likely have been arrested and expelled and she would be alive. In the bargain, the mean girls would have learned the valuable lesson that it's neither right, nor safe, to fuck with anybody that way.

This story is about old-school methods. By many standards it's not right, and might be seen as more of the same, solving nothing. It might even be seen as the recommendation of an irresponsible father, perhaps an abuse victim himself in denial about what happened to him. It would be seen as illegal, unconscionable, and a sign of dysfunction. But there are some, and I almost hate to admit that I am one, who think . . . **YES!** Good old righteous revenge.

Though I know full well that compassion, care, non-violence and peace are the better ways, I also know that if Phoebe were my girl, I'd want to make her oppressors learn a life lesson, one that cannot be mitigated by lawyers, media or money. If suffering happened to be a part of that lesson, so be it. I wish I could have been there with her, for her. I wish she could have known that I had her back. But this is the best I can manage for her now.

My advice to the bullied: Learn to relax in the face of stupidity, fear, jealousy and anger; there will be ample opportunities for practice. Learn to listen to those whose opinions you deem ridiculous. They really do feel what they say they feel. Do not participate in stupid, aggressive activities. Learn to view the fire and ice being spewed at you as signs of pain. And try to remember what that famous Jewish peasant said of those who were executing him, "Forgive them, they don't know what they are doing," while his bullies sold his clothes as he hung there dying.

Implement these things, and, while you're at it, learn martial arts, take boxing lessons, carry pepper spray or,
GET A BAT!

Harvard Square

I began kindergarten at Mrs. Casey's Bartlett School in Arlington at age four, and remained through the fifth grade when my parents moved from Medford to Lexington, or the "sticks" as my grandparents, aunts and uncles referred to it.

"What are they crazy? They're moving out to the sticks for cry-eye!" they'd say, even though it was actually only eight miles from where we had lived, and seven from my grandparents. It was still the farthest away anyone from the family had ever moved. And it threw me less into a new town than it did into a strange state. We ventured out and away from all I had ever known. Fishbowl broke and I poured out into the big blue.

In making this move Joe, my father, stretched the bond and bind he was in with his parents, and this seven-mile journey was the most he could manage.

So, off we went: me, Jackie, Joe, Carol the baby, Mikee on the way, and Joey still off a couple of years down the line. I was enrolled in the Lexington school system, having never before experienced public education. I was nearly a year and a half younger than everyone in my sixth grade class at the Lincoln School. It was terrifying. I felt embryonic.

I once saw a nature film of a newborn kangaroo, blind and crawling out of and up the outside of its mother's belly towards the pouch where it would nurse, and grow, and rest until long after it could go hopping around on its own. I felt much like that little, hairless, pink flesh-ball searching for a pouch, for some kind of hidey-hole. No pouches at the Lincoln School in Lexington though, I can assure you.

I saw kids pushed around and even beaten up in the sprawling fields behind the buildings at recess, a time which had always been a playful respite in a quiet, cheerful backyard on a side street in Arlington. At Lincoln I remember seeing Eleanor Curtis have a full, grand mal seizure on three different occasions while the boys taunted her screaming "COOTIE" in her face and a girl swung at her with a school bag.

Danny Ray Stossel, thirteen-year-old colossus of

the sixth grade, beat the crap out of me one afternoon. He dragged me to the Old Reservoir, where I thought he'd leave my dead body for police scuba divers to find the next morning. I was so upset about my new life that some days I walked through recess with a mouth half full of vomit. Acid reflux at age ten.

I spent that year at school unable to concentrate, doing poorly in most subjects and basically closed for alterations. I was unable to find my spot. Once my mother arranged for a few of my old friends from West Medford to be shipped in for the afternoon, but they didn't fit, just like me, and we didn't know what to do with one another anymore.

The next year my parents sent me to Saint Sebastian's Country Day School for remedial torment. Though for me it was another stint in the electric chair, it was that decision that offered me my first opportunity to experience Harvard Square.

I was driven to school each morning by Mr. Sullivan, who took his two sons and a couple of their teenage friends to Saint "Sebbie's" School for Boys. They lived on the other side of Lexington so my father would drive me to Mr. Sullivan's home where I would slip into the car with the high school boys who were all big, and all Irish. They smelled like kitchens I couldn't relate to. I, an infant-Italian-kangaroo, with absolutely zero sophistication, missed every reference they made each morning, was seen as stupid and immature, and was routinely ridiculed. I felt outlandishly immigrant around these monstrous leprechauns; it was as if I were wearing a Borsalino on my head and dragging a hand-grind organ with a monkey on a leash. These guys had artichokes for brains, and these were definitely not fun rides. Mostly, I stared out a window and practiced holding my breath, failing, at each attempt, to pass out.

The Saint Sebastian's School experience was a disastrous blur in which I was routinely slapped by teachers, continued to learn about prejudice on the worst end of it, and from which I was finally expelled two and three quarter years later. The one bright spot in the nightmare was the trip back to Lexington at the end of each school day, which let out at four o'clock.

My travel routine was always the same, and I traveled alone. Peace at last from the bloody IRA. I'd walk half a mile from the school to the trolley, which eventually brought me to Watertown Square. Feeling lost, I took a bus, that first day, to Harvard Square. It became a route I would not vary.

I had never seen the Square before, and will never forget that moment. I was eleven years old in the first week of seventh grade. I'd felt quite self-contained on the trolley and bus—staring at the book covers in my lap, the scenery, and the other passengers, stupefied but apparently calm, again holding my breath with the stunned look of a sedated animal.

I was shocked by the hustle and life I stepped out into at rush hour on that late September afternoon in 1959. The Square beckoned with the promise of adventure and mystery. In the first minute off the bus, I had already seen faces, clothing, and characters beyond my experience, but not beyond my imagination. I saw people wearing berets, walking without apparent purpose; I saw ascots; long hair on men; a cigarette holder, dangled and smoldering in the hand of a woman who was fat but pretty. I saw a girl gesturing like a dancer to a boy in front of her, and another wearing fish-net stockings and ballet slippers under an enormous black sweater which fell below her butt. My mouth was undoubtedly agape as I gawked at my first look at the beat-generation in the unkempt spectacle of its new beauty. I was no Kerouac but in those moments, I felt genuinely *On the Road.*

I gathered myself, books slung under my arm, and headed to the end of the Square through all the faces and hats, and clothes, and hair, toward a gazebo-like building where I had been directed for bus schedule information. The man inside the structure told me that the bus to Lexington arrived every hour, right across from where I was standing, and that it had just left. "Oh, okay," I said, overwhelmed by the sixty minutes of unimaginable options that lay before me, and began to walk away.

"You can wait in here," he called out, and then added, "I have some candy if you want," brandishing a huge, one pound Hershey bar. Just as I began to move toward him, I heard my mother's mantra echo in my brain: "Honey, never, ever take candy from a stranger." In mid-smile and gesture I stopped, frozen, constipated with the fear of what I had been prepared for those eleven years. All of the macabre elements were present in stark and bloodcurdling relief: "stranger . . . little boy . . . candy . . . come inside." My knees rattled like castanets, my rectum was on the verge of prolapse. I saw his smile and through it I saw his teeth and past those I imagined a black heart lying in wait to corrupt or kill me. With zombie aplomb I said, "No thanks," and turned away, finding myself marooned.

Now, entirely terrified of the man in the gazebo, the people on the walkways, the clothes, the girls, the hair, the berets, and the magnitude of the street, I slowly crept, as one newly born, up the belly of the Square . . . to The Coop.

I just knew, upon entering the Rodin-sized doors that I was home. Here were smells I could relate to. Here, amid the dark wood, the mustiness of antique wisdom, the books and magazines, the saleswomen, the scent and structure, the paper and people, I found my place. Everything smart and weird, and apparently welcoming of my outlandish smallness, my utter lack of sophistication, and my sheer, unadulterated, uncooked youth.

I spent an hour in the Coop every weekday for nearly three years. I devoured everything I could lay my hands and eyes on. I was fed there, and read with Evelyn Wood speed to satisfy my immense growth hunger. While grazing the cerebral fields, I stumbled upon ideas and pictures that intrigued and excited me. I saw Alfred E. Neuman's face on a *Mad* magazine cover for the first time and wondered, furiously, about the meaning of his signature question: "What me worry?" I longed to own a copy for weeks before I had the courage to buy one. *Mad* represented forbidden allure, so much of the Square did. It was my inner and under-world, my cavern, where I could live in peace with those who were different, like I was.

In the first months I had become friendly with a few women working at the Coop who sometimes gave me a place to sit and read, and hang my wet coat after coming in from the rain or snow. Eventually, I even accepted little treats they offered.

I had found the place I'd been searching for, blindly, since the day my family moved. A Coop employee once asked: "Where do you live?" "Here," I answered, and barely smiled. It was the wisest and cleverest thing I had ever said to that point in my life. I thought with immense pride about my comment to her for weeks after. When I'd venture around the Square to the outdoor magazine stands, and other magnificent browsing sites, I was safe knowing I could always return to the Coop.

The bus came at the end of the hour, and I'd arrive home at 6:30, anonymous, with my newfound life tucked in, no one knowing that the Square had become my sanctuary, given me holy shelter, and, as well, had built its pouch in me. Finally, I was expelled from the ninth grade, and my ordeal at Saint Sebastian's ended, as did my formal romance with the Square, my alternative mother and lover, who secreted me, held me, taught me, and gave me place and home and hope. I visit now, some Wednesday mornings, to recall and relive her lush gifts, to give thanks and to hop around a bit.

Carnival

I was twelve in the summer of 1960 and had just eagerly returned to camp for my second season at Great East Lodge in Maine. Early one evening, two counselors took us to a carnival in the back of the camp pick-up. There were nine cleaned-up boys tossed in and bounced down the Maine roads on the way to the fair. Nobody was worrying about spinal cord injuries or kids flipping out of the green Ford F-100. Soon we arrived at a dirt parking area in our camp logo T-shirts, rolled-bottom chinos and black and white high-top sneakers (like the ones JFK wore on the Cape when he was catching footballs).

That summer, I experienced a kind of courtly love with the only girl at camp. It was unlike me, as I was not an advanced kid. She looked like Scout in the movie *To Kill A Mockingbird*, which came out two summers later and reminded me of her. Donna was the daughter of the camp owner who was called Doctor Monroe. He was the ideal man for the job of camp director, a school principal during the year, bald, smiling and massively wise and kind. He hired a group of pretty good guys as counselors; most of the staff were schoolteachers in the regular season. Only one, that I recall, had a terrible temper and frightened us a couple of times screaming at some kid who wouldn't go into the vast, apparently unboundaried body of water which we inexplicably referred to as "The Pond." There weren't any other females at camp except for the nurse, and some ladies who worked in the kitchen, and Donna's mother. Once in a while Donna would have a girlfriend come and stay with her for a day or two. They were cute, but not like Donna.

My heart woke when I laid eyes on her. Being a complete nobody when it came to girls had been tolerable up to that point. But this time I felt the ache you get when longing for something you don't think you can have, coupled with the fear that you'd blow it if you did. I had no idea what to do with her—I was a rabbit chasing a tricycle. I just pined, and longed and wanted to get a hold of her with no good reason except that I wanted to. She was a total peach of a girl—smelled like summer. Actually, as I recall it, everything looked and smelled warm and juicy, not because it was July in Maine or because the air was cleaner then. I think it was the scent of youth. The lax and languid trace of sheer uncooked, unadulterated youth.

At that time I had strange ideas about everything, especially girls. But I was mostly unaware of what I had been lugging around inside me from home, the archdiocese and who knows what all (Hai Karate after-shave commercials probably). Part of me knew that things weren't totally alright upstairs because my ideas didn't jibe with what the other boys had begun talking about. In addition, I envisioned most everything in terms of good and evil, God and the Devil, Jesus and Mary; and my burgeoning sexual sensations were fitted to my peculiar inner world.

I had been punished frequently at home and in school and it was clear to me that I was bad, stupid and a source of endless disappointment. So, my sexual imaginings (under the consuming influence of the priests) were also fraught with scenes of demonic torture and violence, sometimes with sexy she-devils, but also with run-of-the-mill dangerous, puke-spewing, slimy man ones. I must have been quite unhappy, but you wouldn't have known it. I didn't. A fish doesn't know he's in the water until he's taken out of it—it's just where he lives. I was pulling off the heist of the decade, stealing the truth about myself from every encounter. For the longest time I assumed that I was alone in my thinking, but I've come to learn that there were lots of us Catholic boys from the 1950s and '60s who took up residence in those emotional neighborhoods. Finally, we began poking our heads out and catching glimpses of one another on the Internet and learned that we weren't messed up and alone, only messed up.

My psychosexual development was painful and eccentric, especially for an altar boy trained in strict emotional custody and scrupulosity. But I was on track physically, so my body was busting out crying for all those things I didn't want it crying for at all. Even though I had shame-filled concerns about what was on my mind, there was Donna every morning; pretty enough to override my odd imagination. She wore her hair only a little longer than the rest of us, was tanned all over and ran around fearlessly barefoot in the tall grass. A nymph in boy camp, always visible on the edge of activities. I couldn't get enough of spying her from a silent angle. I thought that my summer was going to be a fantastic epic about her and me, but, as my father often warned, I was in for a "rude awakening." Sometimes things go the way you think they will—sometimes they don't.

Being the only female in her age group must have been boring and lonely, but I never thought that then. I thought she was there for me, there to occupy and exercise my little fantasy life. Somehow, I imagined she knew that and reveled in it herself. I believed that she was madly in love with me but was keeping it a secret until an opportunity offered itself for her to whisper the truth in my ear. There would be a symphony of summer night sounds as accompaniment along with a feeling that I might pee my pants. And I thought I was effectively communicating all my weird and pre-sexy passions to her through a hormonally driven psychic-x-ray ability (the very type of thinking which is known as psychotic in adults who imagine having such powers). But to me, the whole jumbled, erotic mind-play was a feast of excitement. I was expecting Donna to be the story of my life that season. I wanted to wrestle in the tall grass with her, and lose so bad I could smell the Maine earth.

I wasn't completely expert in achieving full erections as yet, or a "boner" as we called them then, but the rudiments were in place. I could get a "semi" quite readily, or what's now referred to as a "chubby." And the precursor of orgasm, in my imaginary world, was referred to as the "sugary feeling," and was located in the vicinity of my lower belly. The whole idea of the sugary feeling grew out of experiences I had when I was able to persuade my mother to give me a second spoonful of Paregoric when I was sick or otherwise in pain as a younger boy. Feeling the swoosh of opioid pleasure while lying in my bed was a joy unparalleled to that point in my life. Donna's mere presence and the visions I created of her injected me with the sugary narcosis. The pursuit of that sensation became a cause I'd follow in various forms for almost too long. But, some tiny capacity to desire, and even care, about another person began to develop in a way which had not been there before.

Meanwhile, I was busy shooting arrows and rifles, and making things with gimp and leather and copper on rainy days, and riding horses, and swimming in the Pond on non-rainy days, and following the simple rules, and learning whatever they had to teach us.

We campers went on late-night missions, organized by the younger, more sadistic counselors, to trap mythic, dog-sized, rodent-like, woods-dwelling creatures, the very thought of which petrified us. We played games around the fire in the forest, and slept in bunk beds in rough-hewn cabins fitted for six boys.

As a junior camper the first summer, I had slept in a barracks-type cabin with sixteen boys in single beds. This summer, though, was like having a little home and housemates. It was a time for bigger experiences, closer friendships, and more fun, and along with that, a heightened risk of personal exposure. Everything was interesting and awesome. There was a brightness and enchantment to the nights. And exciting events came easily to me, as the entire camp experience was founded on a deep need for escape from the family room. Being away from home and school were the sole ingredients necessary to make life very, very enjoyable.

In these days, before orgasms and alcohol, before marijuana and pornography, we used our imaginations, and they were as wild as we could let them be. One night, a Playboy magazine showed up in the cabin under a couple of nervous flashlights. I put down one of the Hardy Boys Mysteries while we gawked and made comments about the centerfold, and judged each other's reactions. You had to say the right things about the pictures or you risked enduring a "swear-down." Mostly, I kept my mouth shut because I was afraid that my burgeoning sexual thoughts would be a sure sign that I was not right. I had learned that I was not right in my family and at school and I was dedicated to keeping that information from as many others as I could. I had no idea there was anything wrong with my family and the life they provided, but I had a more than vague growing sense that I was way off.

If you said the wrong thing looking at a nude photo in the cabin, you'd get something like, *Hey, are you a queer? I swear you're a homo aren't you? What are you lookin' at? Look at her tits, will ya? Look at her twat. Who cares about her damn shoes, her make-up or her hairdo? Man you're such a fag you'd be grubbin' around her head lookin' for somthin' to jack-off about.* This was the kind of discredit you faced if anything beyond properly-crafted attention to tits, ass, and fuckin' was mentioned.

All of us were abject virgins to most anything truly sexual, but some boys imagined themselves to be more advanced virgins, and I believed that they were. After all, a few of these kids were actually starting to sprout body hair. The Bible story about Esau has weight. It's always the hairy guys who seem powerful and threatening when you're a kid. In those days, hairy equaled scary. I was as smooth-skinned as Esau's twin brother Jacob. As far as the hair factor went, I was a threat to no man. But there were other ways of developing power.

What we did most of the time to increase our images and blow off steam was learn to swear artistically and beautifully. Flamboyant cursing was the currency of cool in the cabins at night. Your respectability depended in great measure on how well you could swear someone down. A "swear-down" was a spontaneous and lyrical explosion of boyhood machismo, nerve, anxiety and sexual wisdom. *"You're so queer you'd rush up and suck a salamander off just to get alone with yourself for one minute of jerk-time with your mother's panties, fruit-boy."*

At this time, being queer was as unimaginable as having sex with a horse, and the very worst thing you could accuse anybody of being. Everyone was referred to as a "homo," a "queer," or a "fruit" at the least provocation. References to being a homosexual could turn up many times in one sentence; *"You are a queer homo if I ever did see a fag, you fruit."* This treatment was also a sign of intimacy. You could call your buddy a queer or a homo and it showed you were close, trusted each other and could get away with it. The dark and damning power of the accusation could be eclipsed by the light of the friendship. It was a relational law, just like "the angle of the dangle is directly proportional to the heat of the meat" was a physical law. It was, all in all, the main mode of conversation among us boys and once out of adult earshot, the filth would fly.

One night, in my bed the first summer, I got into a processional swear-down in the dark with the other boys. When it was my turn, I jazzed up to a wicked rant, which finally turned on me. I got tongue-tied, lost my place, and said something to actually brutally insult myself in the finale. I was mortified for a few moments during the painful and riotous laughter when a saving voice rang out of the dark, saying, *"You were doing pretty good there for a while, homo, but you kinda lost it at the end."* That made me feel a tad better, but I avoided swear-downs after that and stuck to routine cursing without trying to string too much free-style together.

Nicknames were also exceptionally cool forms of expression and self-enhancement. "Tagging" someone with a name that stuck was a highly prized accomplishment—carrying a good tag yourself was too. Getting stuck with a bad one was a curse as pernicious as a huge nose and tiny chin on a preteen girl. There was, for example, John Rupp who was referred to as "Rup-Ture," which I tagged him with, adding to both of our cool quotients. The tag was an especially good one from the swearing or dirty word point of view (we figured rupture was related to penises and testicles), and John himself loved it. And then there was "Muscle-Ed," who was pure white when he came to camp and crimson after the first few days. He was a complete beanpole with nothing in evidence resembling a muscle. His arms and legs looked like red licorice. The paradox of his tag tickled us senseless and Ed liked it because it made him famous. Johnny Griglio, or "Rat-Head," was a kid from New York who combed his hair in a pompadour style known as a D.A. (Duck's Ass) which was the fashion of the day with certain anti-beatnik elements found in cities. He sported a great funnel of hair which arched up and dangled between his eyebrows like a midnight wisteria blossom. The fact that it appeared on his head in the Maine woods was simply the height of frippery. It took a lot of fuel oil to keep that thing up and running, hence Rat-Head got his tag. He didn't take to it, occasionally threatened anyone who used it, and stood fast and defiant by his hair. He wore it with preposterous aplomb.

Rat-Head just hated going into the water for the daily dip because it would wash away the unguent, collapse the pompadour, and expose him as the twelve-year-old buck-toothed weasel he was. A wiry and tough one, but a weasel nonetheless. He'd start piling his jet-black hair up just as he was emerging from the pond with a comb he carried in his swimsuit. The counselors and half the camp would hoot at him each time he did it, but he couldn't seem to care less. The pompadour was his crown and it gave him special power. Being the Rat-Head became a titular responsibility that he eventually accepted and was finally beloved for.

He was always the first boy to successfully approach a girl from the nearby girls' camp at the two dances staged in the barn each summer. It was with great and anxious pride that we'd watch from our corner of the barn, like a cluster of frozen breakfast sausages, as Rat-Head, oiled spinnaker aloft, floated across the straw-strewn floor in Cuban heels to perform a mating ritual which, we were convinced, could only have been learned somewhere on the dirty boulevards of New York City. He was a miracle in Maine.

I was on the shy side at the dances, but was eventually able to find my way around and would shuffle about in chinos, bumping into one girl or another and calling it dancing. I never saw Donna at one of them so there was always a small sense of disappointment. But still, I looked forward to the dances and had fun, though always with an eye toward Doctor Monroe to see if she might appear to continue my imaginary drama. I think they needed to keep her from the boys, fearing what could develop to ruin the summer for everyone.

We boys were all pretty good friends and it felt exciting and easy that night going to the carnival with still a couple of hours of light left before dark. We pulled up to what looked like an ordinary country fair. I didn't have a lot of experience with such events, but I had been to the Fourth of July celebrations at home and to the Salisbury Beach amusement park at the Boston shore. The smells, sounds, tattoos, excited shouts, and terrified screeching from the carnival rides, the dogs roaming with noses to the ground for scraps of fried dough and tufts of cotton candy looked familiar enough. Also familiar was the over-representation of fat women, and humongous men wearing checkered flannel shirts, beards, with carburetor-stained hands and filthy baseball caps found on carnival attendees no matter where in America they're held.

This carnival, though, had something the others didn't and I was drawn directly to it. For a small price you could enter the "Freak-Show." A man with a loud mouth in a colorful suit stood outside a tent barking about a *"spine-tingling—once in a lifetime opportunity to see the most bizarre human specimen ever born to woman"* waiting just beyond the canvas flaps. There was a gigantic hand-painted sign proclaiming that "Carl the Frog-Boy" would be the sight of the century. The sign featured a toad on a lily pad sprouting a human head.

I was interested, but not yet ready to part with the price of admission, largely because I was worried and agitated. This scene was something my father and mother wouldn't want me to be a part of. I tried not to think too much about my parents in the months at camp, except when writing a weekly letter home, a requirement of camp curriculum, but now they came to mind accompanied by all the saints. I always attempted to do what they wanted. I tried to be good. I imagined Mary, Joseph, and the Holy Ghost floating above the tent, in cloud formation, disapprovingly and telepathically communicating their collective view of the situation,

"This is at least a venial sin, child, verging on mortal. Mortal sin! And you know what that means. The Devil wants you to go in there. These are bad people and this is a bad place. You should ride on the Ferris wheel instead. We already know all about you and the sinful thoughts you use to bore into Jesus' wounds. We will deal with you on that later, but for now, don't make things worse for yourself by going in there. And don't slouch, stand up straight, close your mouth, leave off

picking that thumb of yours, and just stop touching yourself altogether!"

So I was not inclined to go any farther with the freak-show idea, being the good boy that I was trying to be. Plus, I couldn't really stand the impresario. He kept my attention but I resented him for it. This man was a glad-hander like you've never seen. Listening to him was a dazzling affair—I couldn't get a mental breath deep enough to sort through his wall of sound. I couldn't filter the guy out, and remained charmed by him like a flute-dazed snake.

"He hops, he talks, he crawls on his belly like a reptile. Put away your dollar bills and for this show and this show only, everybody gets in for fifty cents. Yessiree, that's what I said folks, half-a-dollar to see the most amazing spectacle you'll see in your lifetime, in five lifetimes." This continued unabated and was, ludicrously, a come-on that finally worked on me.

I was about to do the wrong thing again. My mother constantly chanted admonitions about all manner of humanity; especially those whom she thought did not bathe often or thoroughly enough, those who might carry disease, those who were deformed or mentally impaired, those who had goiters (Lord save us from the unwashed, crippled and schizomaniac goiter-afflicted). And my father was concerned about all of us being "swindled." *"You think I'm gonna let a chump with a*

necktie swindle me? I was born at night, but not last night."
He would rather fork over ten dollars straight away than
order magazines from one of those door-to-door student
salesmen. His theory went as follows:

*"If I give him the money to buy the magazines, I'll
never get them. They'll never come, and he beats me for the
ten bucks, see? Then he wins and he makes a monkey out of
me. This way, I give him the money and I don't want
anything for it. I can't lose. I win, ya see? He doesn't get to
beat me."*

"Pop," I'd ask, "why don't you just tell him you're
not interested in any magazines?"

*"What are you nuts? You want me to come across
like that, like I'm gonna stiff some kid trying to make his
way? You want me to look bad? What'samatter witchew?
Like this, he gets what he wants, the money, and I get what I
want, I don't get swindled and I'm nobody's monkey."*

I knew, I just knew, that being swindled by some
guy with a goiter or other infirmity was in the cards for
me somewhere in the future and I had a feeling the
future had arrived this night.

I don't remember anyone else around. There
must have been someone, a counselor, Rup-Ture,
someone. Rat-Head would have been all over it, but I
was alone. Next to the Barker, on the platform, was a
large basin, about fourteen inches high and more than a
yard in diameter, covered by a white cloth. The guy kept

yapping and then announced that Carl the Frog-Boy was actually in the basin. My attention was piqued and I stood like a post in anticipation of what would happen next. He slipped his microphone under the cloth and a voice croaked, "Hello, I'm Carl the Frog-Boy" from beneath the shroud and gripped my chest.

I felt a chill and stiffened, my breath shallower than an Indian yogi's. The loud-mouthed man had hypnotized me and now I was a goner. I looked around wide-eyed and slack-jawed at the other zombies about to go in, and reached robotically into my pocket, past the white foot of a decidedly unlucky rabbit dangling from my jeans. I produced the silver coins and shuffled forward with the pack as the barker's assistants dragged the basin in behind a canvas flap.

The sun was less than an hour from setting and everything was bathed in a red-orange hue, which, upon entering, shone through the tent walls. Once inside, the barker's rant continued at ever-increasing speed and decibels until I felt demented. Then the dizzying fanfare stopped for a moment of dramatic silence. The cloth was ceremoniously removed—*abracadabra*—and the head of a young black boy floated above the basin's edge. He had short, nearly shaved-off hair, and a dull expression on a handsome and unenthusiastic face. Apart from his apparent apathy, or perhaps because of it, he looked like a completely normal teenager crouching in a tub. The spell broke in that instant and I thought that it was a stupid rip-off, and that nothing at all was going to happen. I wanted to bolt. I wanted my money back. I thought about the ice cream sandwiches made out of cookies I had seen entering the fair, and imagined the celestial Triumvirate, nodding their approval. I *was* going to be good after all.

I did not anticipate what happened next. The basin was tilted upward by the barker's minions and Carl the Frog-Boy spilled out sideways onto the tent deck. The sound of his bare hands, knees and feet hitting the floorboards struck a timeless emotional note, and I vibrated there, in thrall. The vision was shocking and unique. I couldn't take in all of what I saw—his limbs and sinews had been so hideously sculpted by fate that his body was literally twisted into the torso of a smooth-skinned, tailless amphibian. He wore only a bathing suit. He seemed tiny by human standards but positively monstrous as a frog while he crouched there, vulnerable and motionless, looking at no one. The crowd *oooohd* and *aaaahd*, and mumbled. I was dazed, but after a few moments I noticed that I felt lonely and disconnected from the gasping crowd around me. Though I was still right there, I felt sucked out of the scene and isolated. In it but not part of it. I froze. Actually, I was not so much frozen as suspended, as if in gelatin, unable to move, but able to observe my environment.

That moment remains alive to this very day. Right then I experienced enormously competing emotions, hung up and drawn between two forces. One was abject mystification at the twisted wreck of a body. I saw him as incredibly separate from me and anything and everyone I had ever known. The other was a ground-shaking ache and passion for his raw, humble, basic humanity. I saw that he was a boy. He was like me.

It was a moment of empathy that was new and, as it had with Donna, something moved inside me that summer. But, even then, before the very spectacle of his flesh and blood, I knew that what I was experiencing was bigger. I felt on the verge of a great and terrific discovery, one which I was ill-equipped to make use of. Breaking through to new emotional capacities is a necessary and common experience for everyone, especially kids, but it was the sharp awareness of the breakthrough and its subsequent impact that was so stunning. And so, I stood there, transfixed, dumbfounded, frightened and, oddly, impassioned. Stood staring like a fish that had been taken out of the water a minute earlier, one for which the struggle for life had given way to a still and quiet preparation for the end.

The show was soon over. The Frog-Boy hopped around laboriously on stage at the instruction of the barker, and was quickly lifted back into the basin and removed from sight by the assistants. I don't remember exiting the tent, but, in the minutes and hours that followed, I felt knotted-up and twisted inside. I walked around the carnival tense and preoccupied. It is my first conscious recollection of falling into a dissociated state, one that would become familiar in the not-too-distant future. It was the start of a new kind of numbness.

Another camper asked me to go on some rides with him and I did, but I had no enthusiasm for them. He said, "That was great, huh?" getting off of a swinging pirate ship; "Yah, great," was my cadaverous response. But nothing inside me was working in the period following the show. I wasn't myself. I felt a pain and a strangeness inside, as if some bony protuberance might begin to develop and show itself, pushing against my skin to recraft my body, fitting it to its newly discovered interior landscape. It was dawning on me that I, myself, was a twisted being. Yes, Carl *was* like me, very much like me. Becoming increasingly aware of this atomic fact in the midst of the carnival was not comfortable to say the least, and far more than I was able to cope with. I felt like my vital brain chemicals were leaking out onto the littered and matted scrub-grass, rapidly draining me of my former life and alerting me to a disastrous future.

This massive inner shift, which began with seeing the Frog-Boy, continued unabated and tinted the days ahead. His image seldom left me. It replaced Donna's. I felt, for the first time, a concoction of frightening identification and bewildering compassion for someone, and, of all candidates, it was Carl the Frog-Boy. Not my parents, or grandparents, or siblings, cousins or friends—not the priests, or my teachers, not the president of the United States, not the starving Armenians or the prisoners of war, abandoned and dying in Japanese rat-cellars, not the kids with polio or hair-lips. Not the ones I was supposed to identify with or feel compassion for. No, I felt it for Carl. And I felt him in me. This was some kind of madness and a further sign that all my goods were damaged.

I had been taught through countless means that one such as he was to be shunned, not looked at directly, not breathed around, certainly not touched, as one of his skin cells might enter a minor scratch and transform me into an horrendous reptile. The freak show was supposed to be an occasion for witnessing terrible things from a great distance. I was meant to view horror, war, death, and destruction from a flagstone patio, on a television set, with a barbecue sizzling in the background. I wasn't supposed to see or feel anything real. I was to kneel on pews and recite prayers for the Purgatorians and for the other faithful departed. I lived a fantasy existence. The Wonderful World of Disney every Sunday night, with my happy family around the blue television-lit room smiling great dreams of love to one another during the commercials. Then on to Bonanza, and bed, wrapped in cotton-candy blankets of affection and eternal care.

The carnival show offered the populace a chance to see a ghastly irregularity, an objectified being, coupled with an opportunity to feel separate, superior and therefore comforted. *"Poor thing,"* my mother would say passing a crippled or deformed child, *"Don't look at him, honey, it's not right."* She would then walk on, squeezing my hand tighter, confident and secure in her belief that she had a normal child, while I, pulled along like a Mexican lap dog, had already begun imagining sexual and religious phantasms I had no words to describe.

In my connection with The Frog-Boy, I was positioned against all my training and understanding, my culture, the church, my family, and every kid I knew. The fantasy of my dissociated, insulated life was weakened, and it was all I'd had. Again I wasn't feeling the right things, and if I spoke about it to anyone, I wouldn't have said the right things, and would have been flayed by a collective swear-down. So I said nothing. I carried my reaction like a self-administered tag: *FREAK!* That would have been my tag for the summer. Or "Frog-Boy." I would have been publicly crucified—martyred in Carl's name.

The stigma of the Frog-Boy stayed with me. The shift inside continued its course, forming and deforming me. Before the carnival, the only true pity I had felt was for one long dead before I knew of him. I felt something like compassion when I envisioned, which I frequently did, the humiliated and crucified Christ. Jesus of Nazareth had caught my devotional attention four or five years earlier, during my training for first confession and communion. We Catholic kids were encouraged to *"Feel the pain of Jesus and imagine how he suffered for us, for our sins and for our salvation. Feel the nails in his hands and the gash in his side."*

Jesus, I was well aware, endured unimaginable pain and suffering. He, I knew, was stigmatized, but in a noble, sacred and powerful way. In my mind, I would have gladly switched places with him if I knew I was really one with God. It would have been just fine if I knew I was a part of saving all humanity and would be eternally worshipped and adored for having done so. But even without that, I was poised and ready to take on the nail holes and the whip marks every day for his sake anyway. That seemed a price well worth paying. It was glorious, imaginary empathy—the only kind I had known.

But Carl the Frog-Boy was another matter. He suffered pain and humiliation I couldn't begin to understand. He too was stigmatized, and his payoff was fifty cents from a bunch of gawkers and a splintered floorboard to crawl around on. Why had I chosen Carl to identify with? I imagined Doctor Monroe, sadly and helplessly washing his hands in The Pond, wagging his head to chants of *"GIVE US THE FREAK, GIVE US*

THE FREAK!" The truth was that I was already carrying his stigma. I knew I had to keep it all inside. It was a matter of life or death. I was twisted from the inside like Carl was on the outside, and had to keep it a secret. I was now no different from Peter, the New Testament chicken-shit, denying his relationship with Jesus. I had begun to learn, in my tiny existence, that I'd been hiding—hiding myself, my feelings, and the truth about my life, and that I had no choice but to hide. Hiding in every conversation about girls, hiding while looking at every nude magazine, hiding in every encounter with a girl, *hide, hide, hide.*

I felt more and more the way Carl must have felt. I was, like he, a curiosity; one who dances to the orders of others, who puts on a good show, who tries to please, and is yet viewed as strange and weird even by those who commanded the performance. I felt ugly, bad and wrong inside. I realized that I was guilty of thought-crimes punishable by death, or at the very least, deformity, illness and goiter. I was a Hell-destined sinner who would finally be exposed to all as a perverted fool.

I became increasingly anxious and insecure, with lots more crazy thoughts brewing in my head, thoughts far stranger than telepathic communication with Donna. I had relentless images of punishment and imprisonment in dark chambers, which terrified me but, even more upsetting, compelled and excited me. I even began to see Carl as a possible product of Hell itself. A Hell which was populated with lots of Carls and other dark, deformed creatures, transmuted to symbolize their sick sins and then destined to live in Hell's mire under the spears and spikes of wicked she-devils. Carl being only one of my earthly brethren, all of whom I'd eventually meet in my foul post-life retreat.

I longed to be a slave in Hell, tortured by those dark mistresses, somehow managing to keep my grimy pleasure a secret from the King and Queens of The Nether World, and even reveling in my exclusion from Heaven. I wanted to stay in the place of secret excitement, though I was terrified of being there. I imagined eventually befriending the Devil and getting promoted to demon status, sharing the power of evil and control over an infinite number of she-devils who would hungrily do my bidding.

I continued this identification with Carl more than with anyone in this or any alternate world. I had found a personal, living challenge to my defenses and he was the last person I would have expected or wanted to serve in that role. The wound of empathy for him felt anything but glorious and imaginary. It was real and raw and unwelcome and it made me see myself and my life for what it was. Unhappy, fake, perverted, and doomed.

I began inflating my defenses. The Frog-Boy's

deformities were evident. He was unable to hide. I would have to speak about mine for them to be known, something I vowed I would never do. I was safe, I thought. I had carried the deformities inside, in the dark, all this time, all the way from home, and church, and school, all the way into the Maine woods, and to the barn, and the bunk, all the way into every game and conversation, to each girlie-magazine, to every swear-down, to Donna and to the carnival and had gotten away with it. Why couldn't that persist? It had worked so far. Maybe, I thought, it could continue to work—except that I had lost my childish grip on things, my false confidence, telepathic powers, and grand imaginings, all of which were based, I came to realize, on absolutely nothing.

I carried the weight of an invisible bag of defects and sins, which I now felt destined to drag behind me for the rest of my Hell-bent life. My sins and perversions were real, no longer imaginary, rote infractions such as, "I disobeyed my parents, forgot to pray before bed, and said a bad word." No, this was real, dark soul-sludge, and I carried it around with me each day, as my familiarity with the fearsome truths about myself grew: SINNER, FAILURE, FREAK! All the training and preparation I had undergone in the cauldrons of my family and church manifested with nauseating clarity. They were right. It was all true. Finally, once and for all, I was no good. Sinner. Failure. Freak.

Time passed heavily, as did the season, at Great East Lodge, and my days at camp ended forever that summer. Near the last day, I approached Donna and spoke to her, for the first time with more than just a "hi." It was on the archery field while everyone else was getting ready for dinner. I was shy, but I think I let her know that I had been liking her for a while. She was friendly and cute and seemed interested in hanging around. It was important to be with her, as it provided closure to the dream. But Donna already lost most of her appeal to me. She'd become painfully real, as had so much else, and, in my state, I wasn't anywhere near ready to handle a real girl, or a real anything. I was just barely hanging onto myself. No longer a good boy, I was instead envisioning a new inner life, which had gone from the childish dream of eternal happy Heaven to the exquisite pain of endless agonizing Hell.

The next month, I started the eighth grade, my second year at Saint Sebastian's Country Day School for Boys. I was distant and preoccupied, and flopped academically and behaviorally. After failing some classes, I had to go to summer school to make them up. I arrived at ninth grade the next fall, barely, thirteen years ancient, and by spring, was asked not to return. I got my face slapped hard and often by the priests and other teachers who ran the place during the months prior to my dismissal. As much as it hurt, each slap felt justified and nothing compared to what I knew I deserved.

My time at Saint Sebastian's was a blur, in large part because I was slapped too silly to remember most of it, but I recall the ending. The final moments there involved me and my father attending a meeting with the headmaster of the school to get the news that I had failed the semester and was not invited back. Monsignor Flanagan said, in a voice that sounded as if it were coming out of a public address system, "You're a lazy boy. A very lazy boy." I stared at the floor during the proclamation, and was later criticized by my father, as we walked toward the parking lot, for not facing the beanie-headed tub when he said it. The three-minute walk to the car was the longest and worst one I had ever taken. It felt like a shackled trek from death row to the final gurney.

I dreaded the lethal injection awaiting me. The death knell sounded in that Willy's Jeep, which I was always embarrassed about, not so much due to the broke-down condition of the ancient copper-colored tank that it was, but because of the signs for my father's business on each of the front doors, with the company motto: "IT'S OUR PLEASURE TO PLEASE YOU." Those words evoked deep humiliation, as if others would see me as the son of some obsequious merchant bowing and scraping to garner his pittance from the educated wealthy. The embarrassing truck stood there and shouted out to me and to all: *HERE COME THE LOSERS. THE BIGGER ONE IS BAD BUT NOT NEARLY SO BAD AS THE LITTLE DUMMY HE'S DRAGGING ALONG BESIDE HIM. THE WEIRDO, THE ONE WHO JUST GOT THROWN OUT OF SCHOOL AND HAS TO RIDE HOME IN THAT SHITTING FLUNKY-MOBILE!*

On that day I was exposed again as a failure and lazy and bad and wrong, only this time with the certified imprimatur of the academic and religious communities as public proof. No dream world to protect me. No she-demons to distract me from the truth of my corroded, unacceptable, sinful little life.

My father berated me and batted me across the chest a few times on the ride home (something he rarely did) because I couldn't properly interpret a Midas billboard advertisement, which read, "MUFFLERS INSTALLED FREE."

"What does it mean?" he asked in a loud, already accusatory tone.

"It means mufflers are installed for free," I responded, shaking and on the verge of busting out crying.

"**WHAT DOES IT MEAN?**" he screamed and slammed me across the chest with the back of his right arm.

Now in tears, I bawled, "It means they install mufflers free." Again, his thick arm flew across the front seat, this time causing my head to jerk forward, knocking the wind out of me along with an extra issue of tears, which leaped from my eyes to the dashboard.

"*What does it mean?   What does it mean?*" he bellowed, with raging disappointment over what he'd ended up with for a son.

"I don't know," I said quietly. I sat riveted, and focusing on the teardrops moving their final inch down the metal dash to the glove box. Nothing he said or did mattered after that for the rest of the ride. I was safely dead, practicing numbness again for the long road ahead.

When he screamed a moment later, "It means you *BUY* the muffler and they *INSTALL IT* free of charge!" I remember thinking, "I *did* think they gave them away for nothing, he's right, they're all right, I *am* stupid." And life, such as it was, carried on from there.

I was miserable, but nobody could tell. At least it was never mentioned. But it was during this time that I loved and was the sole guardian of a great big dog. Keno was my companion and protector from ages ten to sixteen, at which time he was taken away from me because of some neighborhood shenanigans he'd got into. My parents never told me the truth of where they sent him. Clearly, it wasn't off to the vet for a trim, as they reported the first night he was gone from the house. I fell deeper into despair and was, for a while, disconsolate. The love I had for him remains with me today, and I continue to feel his terrific loss. He visits in dreams every few years and I ask his forgiveness for not abandoning my ridiculous life and dedicating it to tracking him down. In my dreams, he is old, somewhat aloof and disappointed with me, but allows me to carry his great and tired weight in my arms, my face pressed against his dull, ragged fur, and he tacitly forgives me. He was the deepest and most concrete example of love and connection with another being I had experienced to that point. The capacity to feel grew painfully slowly. Being broken open by a frog-boy and healed by a dog was not in the plan anyone could have imagined for me.

Me, puppy Keno,
Mikee in the pen

I was developing some rudimentary awareness of myself and others, as if coming out of anesthesia, still suffering the effects of the protracted psychic surgery I'd undergone. It felt, at times, unendurable, but I began to wake up. And I woke exhausted and weak. But as the fog dissipated, I got more and more angry inside. Anger felt good, alive and powerful. Nobody could tell. I developed massive interests in martial arts, boxing, and many types of conventional and esoteric weaponry. My anger was righteous and I fancied myself an avenging angel, a black-winged avenging anger-angel. I would not be messed with.

During this time of rage, ironically, I grew more and more able to experience other emotions as well. I started to feel deeply for insects, animals, children, and older people; for sad, lonely, fat, and ugly people; for hungry, blind, homeless and starving people; for holocaust families, for black people, for people who cried without comfort, for those who suffered alone and for those waiting to die. I felt for my mother and then for my father.

Life in my late teens was wracked with concern for all of them and a desire to help them. Actually, I did little more than indulge myself, plotting a single-minded course toward the "sugary feeling" for those and many years to follow. I could barely help myself and, for those few years, my dog. During that time, Keno would have taken a bullet for me, while I spent hours fantasizing about putting one into somebody. I was incapable of doing anything truly helpful or constructive for anyone else. Still, sadness and pain over the conditions of others never left.

Over the four decades since, I have worked with a variety of tools and substances, and have been guided by carefully chosen, mostly enlightened, mentors to overcome my history and tendencies and have found welcome, though difficult, experiences of genuine and enduring love. This is, I realize, the carnival prize I won from Carl the Frog-Boy for fifty cents. His living human form forced me to feel something, and to see myself in ways I didn't want to, and might not have, had he not sacrificed himself in the world. He gave me the gifts of self-inspection and self-reflection, the gift of pain and the wisdom of insecurity. I realized that when I saw him I experienced a private Golgotha and that I was touched, in that moment, by the desire of one self to begin another.

I became a psychologist, where empathy for, and understanding of, others' pain, sorrow, and confusion are the largest aspects of my working life. It's still not easy for me, but because of Carl's gift I continue to be more qualified and capable each day. All psychotherapists arrive at the chairs they sit in by some kind of a painful road, whether they realize it or not. Being a therapist starts out as a good defense against your own issues, but ultimately, no one is fooled.

Things began to change that day at the carnival, but I continued to crouch over the pond, like Narcissus did, riveted by my reflection, and would be blind to anyone else, if not for a wrenching away from my own pain, fears and insecurities by the desire to look into another's life. The pond remains inside. But since that summer, Carl sits in the mirror of the pond, distorting my image until it seems more like me.

Slap

At Saint Sebastian's Country Day School for Boys, in Newton, Mass. (where I met JFK), where the halls were filled with paintings and statues of the patron saint—all tragic and bloody, and prickly with arrows, forever dying but long dead—we were slapped.

He was everywhere, Saint Sebastian, waiting there, in the halls and on the walls, for us to join him.

We were slapped. There were telltale prints on our faces as evidence. The Scarlet Hand, tattooed after lunch outside the cafeteria. The shame sign, emblazoned like a brand on chattel, drawing sympathy from those who knew what it meant the hard way, and ridicule from those who wanted us (the Italian-named ones and a few other non-"guinea-wops") beaten down and shunned, those blood-loving Irish-Catholic boys, and their henchmen, the lay teachers; those teachers, who, along with the God-fearing priests, slapped us. We walked past them with our marked faces lowered for fear of getting hit again.

We boys, I remember us: Dennis Romano, Joe Tocco, Toby Accardi, lots of others, and me. They'd choose the kids whose names ended in vowels, or the ones that just looked dumb, weren't cute, or from the poorer side of town (the kids with scuffed clothes and cheap, buzzed-off crew-cuts). We were slapped.

Slapped, like Jimmy, the kid who lived on top of the three-decker next door in the old neighborhood, whose mother jerked him upward by the arm while he, stock-still, was propelled by the force of her rage—her catholic, righteous, fervent rage. He stood, jerked and slapped. And we ran when we'd see her coming—we'd go, "*JIMMY*," in frantic whisper and turn to bolt. He'd freeze, feeling the nightmare growing behind him. Running would be worse for him at the end of the day. We'd watch from a safe distance shielded by hedges and trashcans. Her face, I'll never forget, grinding anger in her teeth and twisting the promise of punishment in her sulfur-lit eyes. Like that, we were slapped, the boys of Saint Sebastian.

All of us confirmed by the Bishop (and they said the Cardinal and the Pope and Jesus himself, as if, were there) and we should be so honored that he ("His Eminence") was coming to enlist us into "The Army."

"*A Soldier in the Army of Christ, boys. No greater honor than to die in Christ's name.*" And then he would slap us—one by one—waiting in line, in the face. The sacrament. The sanctioned and consecrated production line of abuse.

A martyr. How I prayed to be one, to die in Christ's name. Direct line to heaven. Straight shot, right through the heart like Sebastian (through the brain like JFK). Saved from this hell and no stopping over in purgatory even. Center shot. Surefire trip.

Well, we *were* martyrs, weren't we? We were sacrificed on the altar of right and wrong. We, on the worst side of that equation, of good and evil, salvation and sin. True, but still, we were sacrificed while *trying to be good.* Isn't that an essential criterion for martyrdom? It's not so much what you end up achieving, it's what you tried to do—it's your hope and intention that defines your goodness. Every desire of the heart is sacred, every true desire holy, no? Guess not, because we didn't make the cut.

So, me and Dennis and Toby and the others, we never got big bleeding holes like the real saints. Not black-torn bullet holes or red-skewered arrow holes. The real saints had wounds worth remembering and referring to and honoring and sanctifying and emulating and wishing for. What we had seemed like nothing, though they were lethal enough. We had the tiny, cheap holes. It's always the big wounds that get all the attention.

My own wounds and holes fashioned from homemade weapons, battles in the family room, and in the hallway to my bedroom. In the bedroom where the window by the bed was a screen for the nightmare face, which spoke, *I'll give you somethin' to cry about right now. Shut your mouth, shut up, or I will kill you so help me God.*

Little holes, like little cheap rooms left empty, always a fizzing-out neon-vacancy. Little pain-holes, perfectly ready and waiting for the priests to enter with their twin fangs of sin and guilt—leaving behind their brand of God-venom—and filling the space up with shame and rage and fear and death. We, the boys of

Saint Sebastian.

　We were slapped.

　Ears swollen until we couldn't hear. Eyes, red-tear filled, until we could no longer see. Arms jerked until we lost our footing and couldn't walk. They had their reasons, if you asked them, I'm sure. Slapped correctively, slapped for God in Jesus' name, slapped for being silly or loud (or for fun? Because they could?).

　We were slapped.
Like the time I was sitting outside on the stoop in Worcester one summer afternoon years later (stoned probably, daydreaming definitely, playing with my hair) hearing the screaming anger of a woman I couldn't see. Thinking, in the  moment, it was her shrill response in an argument with a man, a bad man, who hadn't yet spewed his wrath back at her, and just then she rounded the corner yanking the arm of a two-year-old boy.

　Dead already, he was.

　I saw in him, me, and the others, and it hit me in the face. She walked past on the other side of the quiet brownstone street (so out of place, though these women did sometimes work the neighborhood), not noticing me at all, and screamed down at him, "**I hate you, I hate**

you," and he walked on his baby legs, in what was a jump suit, but more like a snow suit in summer, because he was frozen, and he was dead. Dead from heart slap and brain slap.

She was so sexy and gorgeous and tilting on spikes and paint and pain herself, I wanted to run to her and say, "I'll take him. Give him to me and I'll take him away. No one will know." But actually, I wanted her to be with me. To turn her evil sex-fangs on me instead. Slaps leave you looking for more of the same. *Lady, whoever you are, you're beautiful and the holes are ready. I've been waiting a long time here. I think I can handle it. Now, I remember everything—dig in, kill me if you can. Kill me.*

But I wanted to take him too, to be with me to love him somehow, to bring him back to life, just take him home to my parents (only choice I had) until I finished college and make him my own. My first birth. And she, the hooker, would be forever indebted and visit me and make me suffer her losses with her eyes and tilting legs as support payment.

I didn't do a thing. Not one thing. I sat on the stoop. I was afraid. Afraid of her and because somewhere deep in the cheap little room I found a note that read, "You'll slap him too." And I'd wind up with her every night as a reminder of what we did. Afraid I'd see a new face in the bedroom window . . . hers . . .

telling me of my guilt and sin and punishment to come. So I remained on the stoop, the pathetic martyr wannabe, licking his tiny wounds, filling his empty rooms with drugs and fantasies of the darkness, which excite.

That baby would be forty years old now, if he lived through his death. I never forgot him. He's still mine. And he's safe. We live together, after all, because slaps leave plenty of rooms inside.

Prayers

My father, Joe, had heard the axiom, "The family that prays together, stays together," on TV and, sensing that the bunch of us were in a mess, got it into his head that all six family members should kneel around my sister's bed while he used the excuse of prayer and the cover of God to air his grievances about each of us, especially my mother, Jackie, in the most thinly veiled, and pious ways imaginable.

And Jackie, so enraged for infinite reasons, both real and imagined, would herself use these occasions to rebut Joe's invocations of divine aid with his sub-standard family, by counter-praying her version of what was going on at the house.

These episodes of worship and religious fervor included tears and shouting, nausea, delirium, and dissociation pretty much throughout the service. If only we had all passed out, the event would have resembled a fundamentalist revival meeting. Unfortunately, we remained awake.

Kneeling around a twin bed was a unique experience. It made us uncomfortably close and kneeling was something we only did in church, facing forward, never towards one another, making it piercingly important to avoid eye contact. Jackie always arrived late, hot from the kitchen, and in a fuss, wiping her hands on an apron. We formed a human moat around the bed—one that would rapidly transform into a sewage drain. If only I'd found whiskey or marijuana back then, I'd have had a floatation device to carry me through it all, but that wouldn't come till the end of senior year when a teacher introduced some of us to pot.

If the whole scene hadn't been so painful it would have been funny.

Even the youngest kids knew the prayer sessions were crap, and mind you, we had all been baptized in the dirty water of Catholicism. I pretty much felt soul sick on these occasions. Just as stomach aches followed dinner most nights, so did a kind of religious sickness follow these prayer meetings.

Joe'd begin booming with the Apostles' Creed, "*I believe in God, the Father Almighty, maker of Heaven and Earth . . .* " With his extravagant volume, the Boston accent and the extreme piety, it was a ridiculous performance that was staged in that hot and tiny room. He was fervently evangelical—embracing the roles of titular, financial, and now, sacred head of the family. He felt he had to don the mantle of spiritual leader to keep afloat the lost and sinking ship of fools and sinners that were in his charge. He was on a tirade when he prayed. Despite his best efforts he couldn't muster any grace. He didn't seem to be trying to save us, but instead, to distance himself, not praying with us or for us, but *at* us—nailing his family to the cross of shame and failure he was constantly constructing. Then he'd bang out the Lord's Prayer: *"Aaah fatha who aaaht in Heaven hallow be dy name dy kindom come, dy will be done, on Eaurth, as it is in Heaven"* . . . and so on all the way to *"and lead us not into temptation but deliver us from evil,"* at which point he'd glare at Jackie.

Here, she'd begin dramatic breathing, and eye-rolling and getting more and more hopped up—and I'd think, *jeez, Dad, dial it back a little.* After that, he'd commence to specific praying about the individuals around the bed and that's when the fun really began. He felt perfectly safe under the shelter of divine entreaty. I mean, who's going to interrupt a conversation with a supernatural being?

Jackie, that's who.

And here, taken from the liturgical notes and

accurate within the boundaries of human memory, is an example of one of the sacramental events:

"*Dear God, please help mummy to be and do bettah.*"

Jackie'd say: "Jo-*oh*, whaddya mean help me? Help me what?"

"*You know what. I'm asking God to help you with your problems.*" (These, I had come to know, were largely related to unsatisfying sexual relations. Big surprise.)

Then she'd fire back: "Hey, pray for yourself, brother. How bout this? 'Dear God, please help Joe to keep his big mouth shut for once in a blue moon.' Hah? How's that?"

"*Jackie, don't staaht, I'm doing the right thing here. Don't you want God to help you?*"

Jackie'd come back: "Don't you want God to help _you_, Joe? You want me to start telling God what _you_ need help with?" (These issues, I had come to learn, were related to particular needs and hygienic matters Joe both struggled with and denied.)

"*Jackie, don't you understand anything? Do you have to turn everything stupid?*" (The very word "stupid," for lots of good reasons, triggered Jackie into a blind rage.)

Now the speaking-in-tongues segment of the service was about to begin:

"Jesus Christ almighty, I'll talk to God about myself—can't I even talk to God myself without you sticking your two cents in?"

"Jackie, what's the matter with you? You say 'Jesus Christ' like that, while we're prayin'? You take the name o' the Laud in vain?"

Now, with the spirit upon her she fires back, "Oh, excuse me, Father Clement." (She called him Father Clement when he acted holier than everybody, because that was the name he'd chosen in grammar school to take upon entering the priesthood one day, and which Jackie swore up and down she wished he'd gone through with.) "I'd miss you kids if he did that," she'd say, "but at least he'd be outta *my* hair and I'd probably have some other kids." This concept of Joe as a priest and Ma with another group of kids would occasionally occupy my thoughts obsessively the way things sometimes did *after* I discovered marijuana.

"Jackieeee, I'm asking God for help with the whole family. You have problems—everybody has problems—don't you want help with your problems?"

"My problems, my problems, Joe? You son of a bitch!" Then she'd scream, "Why don't you go screw yourself!" and start crying, pounding her fist into the mattress.

We kids are kneeling around the bed in the middle of this, as if we're invisible, all of us nervous, trapped and hot.

Right at this point in the service, the cat, who had also been in attendance, would make a hasty exit, tearing around the corner, heading full-speed for the cellar. You can trust animals to have good instincts. Like monkeys heading for higher ground just before tsunamis.

With the evening prayers veering off and running on a grim course, I, as the oldest, would ask something like why we didn't just pray to ourselves, silently, the way we do in church.

Joe could then be heard from the pulpit with his stock answer, *"The family that prays together stays together."*

"I know Pop, but it doesn't say, 'prays *out loud* together'."

He'd look at me, his face twisted with sardonic confusion, and say, *"What's the sense of praying* **together** *if nobody hears it?"*

"It's not good to do it this way Pop, because it doesn't work."

"Oh, so you know more than Cardinal Cushing, more than the Pope himself, you know more than everybody, right Mistah?" (He always called me 'Mistah' when he was winding up to hurl celestial thunderbolts my way.)

Unable to help myself, I'd inflame things saying: "Maybe I do know more, maybe I don't, but one thing I'm sure of . . . I know more than you."

Then Joe would go right for the nuts: *"Why do*

you always have to screw everything up? Y'know, if it wasn't for you, things would be a lot better around here."

Comments like this took me back and left me immobilized for a few seconds, and to my surprise, nobody would ever come to my defense. I thought Jackie might, but she never did. (I wondered if it was because she was hoping I'd win one on my own and she'd feel vicariously vindicated, or if she was just happy it was me getting raked over the coals and not her. I think that she'd been cut to ribbons so often over the years she only had firepower enough to protect herself.)

"Me?" I'd say, "better without *me?* How bout you? You're just doing the same thing in here that you do in the family room every other night—saying how we're all screwed up and you're perfect. Things would be a lot better off around here without *you.*"

"That doesn't even make sense," he'd say, astonished. *"There wouldn't be a 'here' without me."*

That would get me thinking about Jackie's alternate family idea and so I'd say, "Ya, well, whatever, if you don't know what it means, I can't explain it."

"People who can't explain themselves don't know what they're talking about."

About now my sister, anxious, I'm sure, for things to end, would chip in to tell me I was being a jerk.

I'd snap, "Oh yeah . . . of course . . . I should have known—little miss can't do anything wrong. Carol, wake up and stop being a fucking idiot."

Here, Joe would blow, *"Don't you DARE use that language in this house. There's something wrong with you—there's something wrong in your head, Mistah."* And then he'd reach across the bed to comfort Carol. She'd well up with tears and look at Joe with her huge, brown eyes and thick, moist lashes, looking like a kid on an ad who needs food.

The two little brothers would be pretending they were praying, but were actually nervously ducking and giggling into their clasped hands. About here, Jackie'd ask, "Are we done with the prayers yet, Joe?"

Loathingly, he'd reply: *"Carol and I are going to stay—the rest of you do what you like."*

Carol (who has since converted to Judaism) would bow her head and extend her arms and folded hands on the bed in preparation for submission to the divine father.

Jackie and I would leave. (The cat—the smartest in the bunch—long gone.)

The little brothers remained, faces totally buried into the bedspread to muffle their anxious mirth, while Carol and Joe continued with Our Fathers and Hail Marys, and the confidence of the righteous, and blameless.

Deep down, I guess I wanted the prayers to work. I wanted to believe there was a way out of the tension and sadness; I wanted to believe that salvation was possible for my parents, for us. I now think that this was Joe's motivation too. As mismanaged and blind as his attempts were, his intentions were good.

I had heard stories of St. Agatha in Agony (as she is referred to) who died in defense of her purity after Quintanus, the governor of Sicily, tried in vain to get her to have sex with him. She was imprisoned for a month with a prostitute designed to convert her interests, to no avail. Those were some crazy days back then. What must that have been like? *"What ees wrong with hair? But that Agatha she ees impossible. Put hair with the putana and see what appens, eh?"* When that method didn't work, Quintanus turned from warped sensual intent to abject cruelty and had her breasts cut off; she was then rolled over sharp stones and burning coals, and finally taken back to her cell where she died on her knees while praying. I privately adopted Saint Agatha in Agony as our benefactor, because I thought her name was hilarious and because her story was heartbreaking. But she never did us any good.

This was as far as we'd get with private religious practice. The rest of it was Sunday Mass, a public showing in which we were always unfavorably compared to the Irish-American families by way of Joe's grotesque expressions of revulsion along with his embarrassed whispers to us, because the Irish-American parents, all tall and proud, led a flock of at least six, and as many as ten, white-gloved girls and freshly scrubbed and beaming boys up the aisle to holy communion for all to covetously observe.

We never looked entirely presentable despite that being a goal. For one, Joey, the youngest, couldn't keep his clothes on right. His belt was ten inches too long, his shirt was always at least half untucked and misbuttoned, his necktie askew, and his hair spiked in all directions, long before it was the fashion. Mikee, in the middle, bumped and flopped around like a drugged baby chimp, usually lying in the pew trying to sleep. And Jackie always forgot to wear a hat and had to pin a hankie to her head so she looked like she was just in from Romania.

Inevitably, Joe would scan us with a look that asked, *"How in the wide world did I get tangled up with this sack of salamis?"* Carol, of course, was always nothing but beautiful and meticulously dressed. (Upon closer inspection, though, while she didn't quite have a moustache, she was clearly the most ethnic-looking of the kids. Even with that, it must be said, she was adorable.)

And we hardly ever went to communion (Jackie never did. I think she was embarrassed about her hankie-head, and I also believe she saw herself as being in an agonizing and perpetual state of mortal sin.) Joe—I don't know why he didn't go up, probably impeded by the inward, masochistic chant, *"I am not worthy to receive you."*

I, well, I was mildly hazardous. Like, if they had that 'peace be with you' ritual back then, I might have told somebody to back off when they tried to take my hand.

The entire process was a miserable and degrading weekly holy obligation.

After we got home from church, Joe had the awkward idea that he should administer a comprehension quiz on the gospel reading, and the sermon. The five of us would have been a perfect ad for Ritalin if it had been available then. We couldn't focus on a damn thing besides television if our lives depended on it, and I couldn't make any sense of what was being pumped out from the pulpit. I spent most of my time in church seeing red and frightening myself with fantasies of hell and demons. (Once puberty had taken a solid hold though, these were mostly she-devils I was daydreaming about, and I kind of liked them. So that was okay.) But still, I never heard a thing the priest said and basically couldn't have cared less. As far I was concerned, church was another morning in school—just a *religious* occasion to go blank.

In the family room, "Father Clement" would quiz us on the content of the mass, with the thinly veiled goal of exposing how we fell short of his ideal family. This examination fell mostly to Jackie and me. Jackie was not one for tests, having dropped out of the education system before high school (hence, the kook-attack she threw whenever Joe made any reference to her being stupid), and so she'd make something up in the hopes of fooling him. He'd listen for about ten seconds before he'd give her the "WRONG" dumb-cluck buzzer. She'd get so mad she'd bite herself on the wrist just to keep from flinging the tomato sauce she cooked every Sunday all over the kitchen.

Mikee always answered Joe's questions about the sermon in the same fashion, saying: "My views are varied in various ways," just as he quickly exited the inquisition arena. Mike always found silence to be a good weapon, and sleep his best escape, and he used them both as a shield throughout his early years.

Joey could never be found, even with a search warrant, ever.

And Carol would simply bat her big brown eyes, and smile (perhaps knowing her answers didn't much matter because Torah study was in her future), which seemed to work just fine for Joe.

Since I never heard a thing at church, I couldn't give an intelligent answer and would soon be lumped in with Jackie as a Dumb Cluck.

All the family members ended up going their separate ways. I left for Canada a month after my eighteenth birthday.

Joey eventually moved to L.A., where he has remained for twenty years, the last twelve of which have been spent in a wheelchair due to a debilitating neurological disease.

Mike has the same medical condition as Joey and is still trying to sleep any and everywhere, only now he uses an electric cart to get around, has two little kids and an oxygen mask he has to wear at night. Due to these encumbrances, he is unable to exit a room quickly anymore and has therefore been forced to stick around and express his views no matter how varied they may be.

My sister is a semi-practicing Jew, has somehow developed a New York accent, lives in a few homes, has divorced her insufferable husband, and has two indulged daughters, both of whom date beaming and scrubbed Irish Catholic boys. I hear that she's hilarious, is still pretty and has many friends. Jackie and Joe themselves broke up after forty years of marital bliss and Joe died twenty-three years ago at age sixty-one, ten months after they separated.

Jackie's still with us, goes to the same church every Sunday, gets there late, leaves early and always stands, never kneeling, in the back. Still doesn't hear a word from the pulpit, but mouths silent prayers the whole time instead. Finally, she gets to talk to God on her own terms. Doesn't seem to me that He's been listening, though, because He hasn't answered one of those prayers (except for maybe taking Joe early), but the Lord works in mysterious ways, so we've heard.

And so, it seems that 'prays' and 'stays' don't necessarily go together.

Maybe if we had been better at those services Joe led, we would have hung in there longer, and maybe the rest of us would have stayed healthier, or at least stayed in touch. I don't know.

As for me, I've been back from my travels for a long while now, believe in nothing and haven't got a prayer left in me. And, as it's all turned out—I think that's for the best.

Thank God.

President Kennedy's Party

We were going to a dance recital for my sister and my cousin—daughters of identical twin brothers (my father and uncle). All six of us were going from my house and all seven of them from my uncle's. My grandparents were attending too (old, it seemed, though they couldn't yet have been much out of their 50s), immigrants with appended sisters and sisters-in-law, a listing and teetering trail of imports from a generation before my father's, all out for the night (so rare).

They never went out to dinner . . . *Whaddya nuts? Eat food made by strangers? And the money, forget about it!* But, after dining at home, they'd go out to see the grandkids dancing on stage in a school auditorium, proud to be sitting there and to have made it in this country,

America, the country they loved, happy to let other folks see that they had made it, had enough and more, and that their children were doing well and their grandchildren, up on the stage, even better.

I was thirteen that night.

We got there early and saved a row of seats for the imported entourage coming in from the parking lot with their diabetes and walking canes, their strokes, heart troubles, various constrictions, contractions and halting gaits and their human supports, of which we were always a part.

It was not easy for me to be identified as one of Italian descent, with my long name and nose. I was called, at various times, guinea, wop and grease-ball, while my peers boasted immaculate names such as Greg Scott, Lance Bowie, Ashley Green, and Brad Richards. Some had first names that were legal and military like Judge, Sergeant and Marshall. I had a kid in my class named Major Farrell. I wanted to change my names, all of them: first, middle, confirmation name, but most of all, the last one. I wanted to be identified, not with my parents or grandparents, but with the Beach Boys, Cape Cod and the flawless girl, Ariel Scott (who was Greg Scott's sister). But I had no chance of that. I was the Italian kid, seen by some as less-than. No class, no nothin'. Just this monstrous, unpronounceable name and the nose and just about everything but a red bandana around my neck and a monkey on a leash. That's how I felt anyway. I was embarrassed, and ashamed that I was embarrassed. I was also Catholic . . . I was obliged to feel ashamed.

We really were different from the other kids and families. There was a city sensibility about our family. We needed sidewalks and buildings. We didn't look right in the suburbs. The adults always looked like they were about to lose their balance if they weren't standing on concrete. Watching the adult men try to navigate an open grassy field in Italian dress shoes was a vision of slipping, hopping, mincing and general discomfort. To my father, getting some exercise meant taking an extra-long drive into the country to buy an ice cream on a Sunday after mass and macaroni at home. Going swimming at the beach with the extended family really meant floating for the men and bobbing for the women. No actual swimming. My grandfather, an island of a man, floated like an inflated raft as we clung to his legs and arms, the younger ones even climbing up onto his vast belly to jump, or more likely slide, off a mountain of flesh and Coppertone. He never sunk.

We were just not like most of the kids and their parents in my neighborhood and school. They actually swam and boated and hiked and skied, on snow and on water. They wore loafers; our shoes had laces. They drank cocktails. My family was all teetotalers. Those kids were tanned and windswept; we were white as sheets because we worked for the family business on weekends and in summer. The classy kids looked tousled and ragged, whereas we, progeny of immigrants, were always being made to look respectable, with our hair cut short. To top it off, in the *Boston Globe* they were the judges and the politicians. It was always the Italians who were in trouble in the newspaper. Cosa Nostra, Mafia. With those stupid nicknames like Danny "The Chooch" Cuchinello, Louie "The Lump," Jimmy "The Nut" . . . So, my family being all Italian, and having a few bucks, plus owning a liquor company, it was widely believed that I was a Mafia son. Of course I always said it wasn't true, and that, of course, would be the right answer no matter what the truth was. My denials didn't help matters.

About all I had as a source of pride in my culture was the vague reputation of being in a "connected" family, and I think we may have even played that up a little. With it came the power to make us feel, *hey, we may be guineas but we could be dangerous.* And of course, it wasn't true, *as I have said.*

That night, in the auditorium, we came face to face with the normal, active, fit and law-abiding populace. At the end of the aisle we had claimed appeared a delegation of the others, the locals—the real citizens, the ones who call the cops when there's trouble.

The "Ameriganas," as my grandparents might

refer to them (not disrespectfully, but to acknowledge the differences between those born to the bounty and good fortune of this land and those who fought hard to get in line for a chance at it). These folks intended to occupy the rest of the long row we were in, but my uncle said, "Excuse me, we are saving these seats for other family members who are coming in soon."

The lead American, huffily and with impressive throat-clearing and immense inflation, shifted purpose, backed out of the row and resentfully ushered his family and friends to the row behind us. My father, occupied with assisting the elders, who had just entered the building, missed the interaction. When he came back to our seats and took his place beside me, he must have felt something in the air or read something in his brother's face (it is said twins have a certain clairvoyance between one another). He leaned forward to look down the row and gave my uncle a questioning glance and gesture. I saw my uncle shake his head and finger to say, *it's nothing*. And as my grandparents and other older relatives came hobbling into their seats, the head American, sitting right behind my father, said stridently, "Well, here comes President Kennedy's party."

My father cocked his head briefly, put a picture together in his mind of what might have transpired moments before and, with a deliberation I was unprepared for, turned in his seat and said very quietly and directly to the man who was two feet away, "I don't know what happened here between you and my brother but whatever it was, he was right. So it's best if you keep your comments to yourself for the rest of the night, okay?"

I was frozen.

"Really?" Replied the commander-in-chief, derisively and to the great amusement of those sitting beside him.

Now I turned, holding my breath, to see my father maintain unmoving eye contact with the man. In that moment, I saw my father smile a smile which did not include his eyes and which must have carried a clear and powerful message that we had overcome many obstacles to get into this line because not another word was heard from America that night.

I guess the man wasn't sure if it was words only from my father or if there was something more behind those words—if behind his smile he could see my father's teeth. I wasn't sure either . . . but in that moment, and for all of that night, I felt proud to be sitting in our row. Proud of my complicated name, crisp white shirt, short hair and shined, tied shoes. My father patted my knee, and squeezed it as we turned to the stage to watch the new generation dance.

Fallen Angel

In September of 1969 I rented a house near Halifax, Nova Scotia, with two guys I didn't know well, Reggie and Sheets. They had been high school friends in Toronto, and were students and football players at the university I'd been thrown out of the year before. We ended up getting together, mostly because they needed a roommate, and we discovered we shared a love of girls, drugs and blanket stupidity. While they went to school I was employed as a roofer and became member N$\underline{\circ}$ 291116 of the Sheet Metal Workers Union.

We lived close enough for me to walk to the job at 6:45 in the morning. In the first week, I was instructed to fill large burlap sacks with gravel, while most of the men—older, rough-looking guys with lots of missing teeth through which they smoked roll-yer-own tobacco and poured whiskey and beer—stayed inside keeping warm with cigarettes and coffee. Maybe it was an initiation or something, but it quickly dawned on me that I was often alone filling and loading the bags of rocks. Then we got on the trucks that took us to various job sites. Not a lot of conversation was exchanged in the first couple of days, but during that time, I heard them refer to me as Hipp (for "Hippie"). I don't think the crews knew what to make of me.

I had no money. A foreman even fronted me a few bucks for lunches to hold me until my first paycheck. I couldn't afford the hard hat we were supposed to wear, so some of the workers, under the foreman's influence, showed colossal goodwill by pitching in a dollar each to buy me one. A couple of days later, they presented me with a yellow hard hat with the stipulation that they could write what they wanted on the front. With a wood-burning tool, they engraved the four letters H-i-p-p. It was my name for the rest of my tenure. Those guys thought it was a great curiosity and amusing spectacle to see me in the hard hat, hair flowing all around, sporting my nickname and what they considered to be my entire identity, up front. Most of these men were older, and they lived in a world that was both fifteen years ahead and fifteen years behind the one I was living in. We occupied the same space, but our hearts beat in different times.

I think they were fascinated with me because they'd never seen someone like me up so close. As they got to know me in the first week or so they'd say, "Hey Hipp, them hippie girls fuck like fuckin' rabbits once you get 'em on the dope, eh?" They were always dying to know about drugs, the hippie esthetic, hippie girls and hippie sex. There began an ongoing investigative interview. They were amused by my Boston accent and some of the ways I described things with it. Essentially, I was a curiosity for them.

I had lots of experiences working that job. I learned how to build tar-and-gravel flat roofs. I learned how frightening it could be to fall off the top of a building. I saw my first dead man in an unexpected place, and I learned what it was like to be with a bunch of Canadian construction workers in the middle of the woods during winter after you just got them all stoned off their asses for the first time.

One winter day on a rooftop, they asked, as they often did, about the effects of marijuana and I told them I had some in my pack. They asked if they could try it, and when I said yes, they immediately pushed the crane and winch off the roof so that supplies couldn't get up to us, thereby stopping the job. The guy on the ground who ran the tar pots had to drive back to the office and get another rig, and that gave us more than an hour.

We built a large, dome-shaped shelter of Styrofoam panels connected by duct tape and sat inside for protection from wind and cold. I just passed the bag around, since they all had papers and knew how to roll, and suggested they make very thin individual joints. They were delicate with the pot, like they were holding the baby Jesus, and started giggling like little girls even before a joint was lit. We began in unison and I told them to inhale deeply, hold it in a while, and to smoke the entire joint. They did as instructed, as if in thrall to their personal representative of an American cultural phenomenon. I was Woodstock and the Revolution to them, a sexual, consciousness-expanding rebel. It was great being Timothy Leary for a moment. I told them they had to eat the roach while the ember still burned and they took this final act as an induction to a world they'd only heard about or seen on the news. Most of them got wrecked immediately and were laughing and dancing around, making sexual gestures with their hands and pelvises like aboriginals from an equatorial rain forest. It was quite a show.

I was, of course, being interviewed during the merriment: *What happens next? When does it go away? Will I be able to get hippie chicks now?* And so on. Then the guy came back with the replacement equipment; they pushed that off too. He started yelling up to us asking what was wrong, but the job was closed down because of bad luck, and my image on the crew was forever changed. "Hipp's great ain't he?" they'd say. "He's fuckin' dem hippie chicks left and right, eh? Good 'ol Hipp. He's a smart one even though he's always on the dope."

It was lucky for me this drug-induced transformation occurred, because not long after, a younger crew guy, whom I didn't know, got into a beef with me about something or other, and a fight was brewing. You don't want to be in the woods, on a roof, in a fight. This thug squared off and called me out. I told him I'd kill him like I meant it, but I knew, even as I said the words, that I was dead. He was older, tough and wiry, a hard-working, poor kid from a lousy neighborhood. He was all bones and sinews, his teeth half gone at age twenty-five. The kind of guy who could punch a cow in the side and knock it over. He rushed me when I was ten feet from the edge of a six-story building, and as he did, I threw myself down, clinging to the roof with my gloves and the toes of my work boots like a cat splayed on an ice-pond, determined to get ahold of his leg as soon as he got close enough. His attack was cut short by crew members who escorted him to the ground level. Others brought me down and persuaded us to shake hands. I was sure they'd saved me from falling to my death; I didn't think I would have died alone, but that consolation seemed insignificant at the time. I was shaken up and grateful. Getting high on pot with others has always turned out to be a good thing in my experience.

Though I worked full-time, I remained, essentially, broke. The housemates and I never had money for anything much. We ate almost entirely out of cans; everything, including vegetables, was consumed from cans. Cans, and then pasta and sauce. We called it spaghetti or macaroni back then, fifteen years before the enlightenment, when it became "pasta," and grapes became "varietals."

The house was in a small town called Spryfield about five miles outside the city and sat next to a little pond. The whole area was not exactly a dump, but it could easily pass for one if you looked close enough. There were no lawns, or anything even like a lawn. The small deckhouses were surrounded by hard-packed dirt and stones and some had gravel scattered around them. There were neighbors but we didn't see them often. Once a neighbor gave us a couple of fish he'd just caught and Sheets grilled them in a pan with butter. It was a big deal. Fish, spaghetti and a can of veggies.

Our landlords were pious holy rollers who belonged to the Seventh Day Adventist Church, and went to services on Saturdays where they washed people's feet, couldn't wear jewelry, drink alcohol, dance, play cards, wear makeup, or listen to any music except probably for Seventh Day Adventist hymns. To me it was written all over their faces that they were gonzo. But they were very simple and sweet people who seemed quite old to have a child as young as the one they had.

They lived in the basement with their daughter who was a heavenly beauty of about sixteen. It seems they used to live upstairs in the main house where we were living, but renovated it for rental income while they withdrew to the cellar. I'd been down in their place a couple of times in the year we lived there and it was all dolled-up compared to ours; colorful, packed with objects, lots of religious stuff, comfy furniture and folksy appliances. It was like a little home-in-a-hole. That young girl of theirs was really something and it was difficult to imagine her living down there with her old-ass, religious parents like they were rats in a box. Apparently the Seventh Day Adventists believed in fucking at any age as long as, finally, you made a kid with it and kept that child for God and God alone. And since they lived halfway in the sticks there wasn't much chance of temptation for that poor girl. Till we came along.

When they rented us the house, the landlord mentioned that no drinking was allowed because it was against their beliefs. They never said anything about drugs. Somehow this was not on their radar. We told them we were college boys just trying to get through and that we were not drinkers. They thought we'd been sent to them by great God almighty and that their prayers had been answered. As it turned out, some prayers were answered, but not theirs. We started right in lying to them because of course we did drink and definitely smoked weed all-day and tripped on acid and mescaline on the weekends. And I wasn't really a student, either, because I'd already taken to the workforce since early summer. I was doing time in the cafeteria of the very school that threw me out. Collecting money at the cash register from summer students who once were my peers and now saw me as a kind of loser who'd only ever be a high school graduate, and what a shame that was, what with being a Yank and all and probably coming from a nice family. Canadians, always trying to put a positive spin on things.

We had girls up in the house as often as we could, went and found them and brought them home from any and everywhere. "Stack 'em up like firewood," Sheets'd say. I once saw a girl on a TV ad for a big downtown department store and then, there she was, at a party I was at. I went over to her and told her I recognized her and had been thinking about her since I saw her on TV. We talked a little and then started going out. She was the first black girl I ever dated. She was almost as tall as me and was an exotic-looking model. I felt lucky, and proud to be breaking another cultural taboo. The landlady saw me coming in with her once and just said "Lord!" under her breath. Regular invocation of the divine, I learned, is common among Seventh Day Adventists.

The work crew thought I was some kind of wild-man anyway, and when I told them about going out with Delilah—"Jesus jumpin' Christ on a crutch, Hipp, now you're dancin' with a blackie. She must fuck like a fuckin' rabbit once she's on the dope, eh?" They meant no harm.

Me, Reggie and Sheets were drinking plenty of beer, they more than me, but, at four bucks a case of 24 bottles—Ten Penney Ale, Moosehead and Schooner—it was worth it, and there'd be cases of empties out in front of the house every week. The landlords never said anything except once, and we told them that we weren't drinking but that others would bring beer and we felt bad telling them they had to leave their stuff in the car. That seemed enough of an explanation for them.

What with the girls, the music, and the general depravity, we kept that house in an uproar while those poor people huddled in the basement. We had to have been making a hell of a racket. The main chair in the living room had no legs and we were always slamming down into it. It was a huge, cushy recliner-type, but legless because the bottom had been removed. It looked very weird and was even stranger to sit in. Next to it the sofa seemed gargantuan so we took the legs off it too.

After that things in the living room started looking Japanese. All this alteration made the coffee table too high for the furniture, so we then had to cut the coffee table down to size and kept miscalculating till we almost got it too low. Eventually, it seemed, we'd bring everything down to ground level, and not just the furniture.

Once, from too much fucking around, we pissed an operator off so bad that she and her friends at the phone company made it so the phone rang all the time. We went out of our minds, so we left it off the hook for hours. When we wanted to make a call later that night, we pressed the hook down and it immediately began ringing nonstop. Not a normal sequenced ring, but incessant ringing. The three of us became paranoid because we were tripping anyway and we stood there, frozen, in our kitchen, staring at the possessed phone. It was two or three in the morning. How'd they not know downstairs that wicked things were going on upstairs?

Those landlords couldn't have been too smart to begin with, renting to three obvious freaks. Two of us had hair past our shoulders and Sheets (who was actually not playing football because of a car accident which cracked his head open and almost killed him four months before in Toronto) had his head shaved with a big seam of scar tissue embroidered into his scalp that went from his hairline to the back of his head and made him look like Frankenstein or some kind of sewed-up goose roasting in the oven. And that's to say nothing of how stupid those folks had to be to sign up for a religion that was designed to suck any possibility of fun out of life. Where do people get these ideas? Maybe it's to feel safe. I could maybe see that because I once thought of going down to their apartment when I was paranoid on acid, thinking the normalness might ground me, but I didn't go for fear of getting worse from freaking them out. Or that they'd pull some weird relic out of a closet and start doing a hideous dance to convert me to the Lord.

We played the Jethro Tull album "Stand Up" on a terrible record player and when we weren't doing that we were blasting the black and white TV we rented by the week until the Canadian flag was flying and "Oh Canada" was honking all broadcasts off the air. We were busy day and night doing the devil's work and right downstairs were the God-fearing do-gooders and their spawn. I tell you it was beyond poetic. Good and bad in reverse. Hell up top, heaven down below.

As it turned out, that girl was down there trapped and fantasizing about the twenty-year-olds right above her who were doing just what she'd always dreamed of doing and I for one (and I know I wasn't alone) was upstairs thinking about getting her creamy young breasts and ass in close view without getting caught. We figured there had to be a way to help her get a day pass to perdition with the three little devils.

Her name was Grace. We saw her here and there, coming and going, from our windows above. Her hair was long and auburn in color, always tied back in a loose ponytail, her skin flawless and pale. She moved gracefully; she was slight and tall. She was a true flower in an era of flower children. But Grace did not have flowers in her hair, though they would have suited her. She did not have a peace symbol painted on her cheek, though her face radiated tranquility. She seemed as luminous and pure as all the love everybody was singing about back then. She'd slink around once in a while to say hi when we were pulling in or using the staircases, which were on both sides of the house. One of them led to our kitchen and was above the entrance to their hovel and the other let into our living room.

One day, when her folks were off praying, foot-washing or doing other errands, we saw her by her entrance and invited her up. It was early spring and the air was warm enough that you could smell the muddy earth into which our jalopies were gradually sinking. We were anxious, excited, and already stoned and there commenced a four-person party replete with the four main ingredients: pot, beer, music & the scent of budding beauty. The three of us ushered her up the stairs looking at one another as if we'd found a gemstone in the damp gravel.

It wasn't like we were trying to make monkeys out of these nice folks, it's just that we had to do what we had to do. Normally, if people start talking about God or Jesus I either go blank or verbally attack them. I didn't have any such reaction to her parents, so I assumed they were the real thing. True believers. And I suppose I respected that about them. Anyway, none of the three of us would do anything to harm anyone on purpose unless we had to. I did feel a pang of guilt as we huddled around her and climbed the stairs. I felt a little like a vulture waiting to eat the baby of people lost in the wilderness. I guess I knew, even then, that when the zipper opens, the heart often closes.

We asked her if she'd ever had a beer. She hadn't. We asked her if she'd ever smoked pot. Again, no. We asked her if she wanted to try either of those things and she said, "Please."

Jethro Tull began to spin on the turntable, rocking the walls and floor and we popped open a Ten Penny Ale and poured it in a glass for her. She gulped it down as if she'd never see another. She would. She saw another two. She loved the music, and after the first beer began to move to it. I thought she would cry, she seemed so happy. I couldn't understand how she was able to abandon herself to the action with no sign of worry about disobeying her parents, offending God, or getting misused by us. But, she was cool. And so were we.

She listened to the album three times, always begging us not to take it off to play another. It was as if she wanted to memorize it, engrave it into herself because she didn't trust she'd ever get so close to those sounds again.

When she smoked the pot, she coughed and choked but finally got it in and kept it in. After a few tries, she was stoned and danced and sang to the songs. It was as if she had become the entire Age of Aquarius. She hugged us and kissed us and told us she loved us. We returned her joy and affection for those couple of hours. We didn't realize how far gone she was. We were pleasantly buzzed while she was in Wonderland.

Once we noticed how much time had passed, we wanted to get her out and downstairs before her parents came home. She resisted, but we persuaded her that it was better to leave sooner than later. We walked her to the landing off the living-room side of the house, as far away from the cellar entrance as we could get. The four of us stood there saying our goodbyes when, before we knew it, she flipped into the air and out of our grasp, then fell down the ten wooden steps, landing in the mud and stones at the bottom. It seemed it was in slow motion. The three of us were left there rigid with shock, as we watched, helpless as she cascaded, arms and legs flailing. It was spectacular, as falls go. If you saw it in a movie, you'd swear it was special effects.

We stumbled down after her, asking if she was okay. She was groggy, disoriented, and dirty. We supported her rubbery body back upstairs to assess the damage and clean her up. She was fine, a little bumped and bruised, but okay. After a while we escorted her down the other set of stairs to the door of the basement and persuaded her to drink some water. We recommended she go to bed and tell her parents she was feeling sick and tired.

We were freaked and hoped for the best. On high alert, we waited for her parents to arrive and when they did we were crouching near the window like squirrels. The house was never so quiet unless we were asleep, but this was late afternoon. We never heard a word about it and she never came upstairs again, but gave us exquisite smiles and knowing glances after that day.

The next month, I left suddenly, driving my questionable Karmann Ghia back to Massachusetts. I'd had too much tripping and began to panic about my life. I heard a radio report of a major fire in the city, where families had lost everything but their lives. I called the station and donated all I owned, bed, bureau, everything but essential clothing. I then told Sheets and Reggie I needed to be off. They were surprised and sad. I left them whatever money I had and kept only enough for food and gas home. I called Mr. Albert Grainger, the job boss and said I wasn't coming back to work.

That summer I worked for my father's business, took courses at Boston College and then enrolled in school the next fall to start my life anew. I had plans and dreams and, as the constitution promises, was in pursuit of happiness, which is my right.

And though few of those dreams have been realized, I'm happy I helped a young girl, and some good old boys, to fall a little bit, and was fortunate not to fall all the way down myself.

The Head (or *I Dismember Mama*)

I am going up a hiking trail in Bar Harbor, Maine, on vacation. At home my mother is dying. I know this because she's been going down for a while and because since I woke I've received frantic texts and calls from siblings about my mother's ever-shifting status and their plans regarding how to handle the details of her vigorously anticipated funeral.

I'm all twisted and angry inside, partly because I'm here in the lovely vacation sun and she's there, and I feel anxious and guilty because she's surrounded by the rest of the family and friends and hospice types, but also because I can be like her—restless, overwhelmed, rage-filled, critical, even brutalizing.

These disturbing parts of me need regular

feedings to stay alive, and they need to stay alive because they form a vital link that I have with my mother. If these parts of me die, so does she. Gotta eat. Now I'm facing her death and I have no idea how to handle the impact that event will have on the internal, psychological, emotional link I have with her. That's a lot of hocus-pocus isn't it? Mumbo-jumbo. But somewhere in there lies a truth. Mothers and sons . . . truly, what can you say?

Here in Maine I pass many people who are coming *down* the trail. All of them seem like happy, healthy, energetic, attractive, in-love Americans, and many from other countries, like Canada and Spain. They say *Hi* and *Hola* and *How's she goin' there, eh?* as they pass, smiling, bouncing along.

I'm with my eternally positive and hopeful wife and our twenty-pound Border Terrier. My wife already knows I'm going to the dark side, having been tipped off when, as the mountain first came into view from the highway, I said, *I just want you to know that if that thing in front of us is what you're referring to as a hike I don't want any part of it. I thought this was gonna be a stroll, not a crash course in extreme sports, okay?* She didn't respond, to her credit, and I later learned that in that moment she was trying to find her *happy spot* and mustering her centering abilities to deal with what she knew was to come. Which was my mother, in the form of her husband's body.

Sometimes my wife can freeze emotionally, sort of laminate herself, when I go in this direction. But she doesn't, and tells me, when the hike is over, that she was "inhabiting the body." Something she learned from meditation, yoga and all those books she reads. She said that on the trail during our ascent, when I was in the worst of it, she was feeling every footfall on the path and experiencing each as a little prayer or meditation in itself. Each rock and boulder like a bead on her mala or rosary.

So, she was both loving me and letting go of me, in the best sense of those notions, on this perfectly gorgeous day, on the mountain trail, with all the happy, healthy people. My wife has never been one of those people who love you without measure, soon to hate you without reason. She is balanced and steady. And my dog, always with us, is a delight to all who encounter him. He is so much like her. Positive, hopeful, beautiful, able to love with senseless abandon and also able to let go gently when things turn in a direction he might prefer to resist. He's also one who can numb himself right out, though. Pretend he doesn't hear or understand you when you know damn well the infuriating little brat knows exactly what's what. They fit so perfectly together, and with everybody else here.

I, alone, am the twisted wreck on Cadillac Mountain. I am dark. Nothing's right. It's hot, steep, difficult, my back and hip ache, I am overdressed and sweating abundantly from all the lobster and wine consumed in the past three days, I am sneezing, there's a bug somewhere and I believe there's a tick on me. Older people seem to be bounding past. To this point on the outing, I hate life and am envious of the dead.

Something in me feels homicidal. Need fresh blood.

I once heard a killer interviewed about having murdered his mother. He cut her head off as well, and put it in a bowling bag. This was part of a special on TV about serial killers and other spectacular murderers. In the end, this beheading, matricidal maniac (bowler, I guess), couldn't say why he had done it. He'd lived with her for years, was incredibly tied to her in ways from which he could neither extricate himself nor endure, and apparently got some information, from his own head, that she needed to die for him to live, and so he obliged. Stabbed her repeatedly, then hacked her head off her neck and stuffed it into his bowling bag.

I imagine him as then putting the displaced bowling ball on top of her neck, as a kind of replacement, while her torso lay on the bed where he killed her. And you just know that before the head went into that bag, he had to look in the mirror, at some point, holding her head in front of his face just to see what that would be like, saying things such as, *Carlton, Carlton, where are my cigarettes? I don't see them here. And where's my salami? Didn't I tell you to get me that salami I like? Can you ever get anything straight? And by the way, where's my change? Carlton, Carlton! How many times have I told you to get those handcuffs off the floor? I'm likely to kill myself tripping over that mess. CarlTON!*

I've sort of done that. Looked in the mirror and had imaginary conversations with my mother, her head obscuring mine. I think there may have been multiple murders in that mirror. Or maybe I just felt trapped in *her* mirror, where the light, always bouncing off her, illuminated some part of me that she wanted to see. I can't figure the calculus of it.

Now, back at the crime scene . . . after the killer's little mirror-puppet-show was over, when he finally stuffed the head in the bowling bag and walked out of the apartment carrying it, he saw two happy, young lovers on the landing of the adjacent apartment. They paused and kissed. He stood there watching them, and then he tells the television interviewer, *that was everything I ever wanted right there. A girlfriend to be happy and in love with, and I'm looking at my fantasy, my dream, just a few feet away, and there I am with my mother's head in a bowling bag. I saw what I really was and what had happened to me, and my mother had to die for all that to come about.* It was one of the most poetic and provocative things I'd ever heard a killer say.

So, there I am on the hiking trail with all these off-puttingly happy people passing, with my joyous dog and still hopeful wife, who is practiced and skillful enough to continue to feel her body in the midst of the pall I've cast over the north east coast of Maine. While I feel as if I'm carrying my mother's head in my daypack. This is a small backpack that cinches around the waist and can also be slung over the shoulder by a padded strap. It even looks something like a bowling bag.

My wife knows that I carry my mother with me, especially lately as she's been going down. She doesn't know the head is in the bag though. It is. It spins in there, the eyes flash, teeth gnash, it spews vulgarities. *Fuck this. Fuck that. Fuck you. She's fat, he cheats, you can't do anything right.* It's a whirling dynamo of fear and rage. It needs to feed to stay alive. And it's starving. It's burning up the trail, hungering to disembowel my fellow hikers but aiming for my wife and dog, because they're the closest and most vulnerable source of food. It has to sustain itself, to keep the bond with me alive, in order for the legacy of devotion and pain to continue. But because of my wife's loving heart, and my not-quite-buried gratitude for it, the head continues to just miss its mark. I let it eviscerate only *me* for the time being. A familiar meal. Eaten up inside. And I only say to my wife that I'm okay and to leave me be with my sighing, eye-rolling, grunting and present danger.

In actual fact, my mother's head would not make a good bowling ball. Or, I should say, I'd never replace her decapitated head with a bowling ball. Now, for some people it might work. People with big round heads or faces, say. People with solid, hard and thick craniums. And the finger and thumbholes in the ball might work well for someone with a big head but small, tight little facial features. That pinched look you sometimes see.

So, the bowling ball head-replacement might work for some, but not my mother. Her head looks more like something you'd see hanging around the hut of a headhunter in New Guinea. The folks that are headshrinkers. They create shrunken heads as trophies of vanquished enemies, where they remove the bony structure of the skull and keep just the skin of the face and scalp and then cook it down into a reduction of the original features, making it into a kind of miniature and grotesque mask of the person. That's more my mother's look at this point in these final weeks of her life. So, you definitely would not need a bowling bag for head-transport. Actually, you could leave my mother's place with her head in a plastic sandwich bag, or in a jelly-jar, or pinned to your hat as a kind of a gag-chapeau from a souvenir shop in New Guinea. You could even have it bobbing in a glass snow-globe. Still, no matter what container you placed it in, it would completely suck seeing those happy, kissing little love-birds right in front of you while you were carrying your mother's severed head, in whatever form.

That's what it was like for me seeing all those bright, active people on the trail and feeling the luminous presence of my wife and dog while my mother was dying and I wasn't there.

I was like that killer on the mountain trail that day.

Now, my mother is riddled with tumors. She's tiny, frail and in pain some of the time. But she's unchanged . . . even worse actually. It's incongruous—that all that rage and negativity can still flourish in such a small package. The body wastes away but the spirit does not fade, and if you start out with the spirit of a succubus, it can remain as wild, frenetic and mad as when it was hosted by a strong, healthy, beautiful body. The body I bonded with. The one I loved. The one that began devouring me as soon as I emerged from it. Now, though merely a husk of that body, there remains the force of fury that could wreck a town like the 50-Foot Woman did, in that B-movie, when she got pissed off at her cheating husband.

And we've tried everything. Mood stabilizers, tranquilizers, and anti-psychotics, along with pain medication—the best modern medicine can offer. Nothin'. But, then again, would you give pills to the Devil to straighten him out? It'd be silly. *Ah, excuse me, is the prescription for the Prince of Darkness ready? I'm here to pick it up.* No. We are what we are on the inside and you can dope it up but you can't take it away.

I think she's manifesting Chihuahua Personality Disorder. (I just made that up.) I take this syndrome from that well-known Mexican speck of a canine with the fierceness of a Doberman on bad day. That's my mother.

Eventually, we reached the peak of the mountain, my wife moments ahead of me. I saw her, breathless, over the view of the sea, my dog blissfully running around. We were alone up there. I was awed by her ability to be open to the brilliant beauty even with all I had been doing to cloud and erase it. And in that moment of seeing her, I felt the energy in the bag begin to quiet. And as I moved toward her, I saw my dream of love and happiness and everything I always wanted.

I was not the killer.

My mother was dying, true, but she didn't have to actually die for me to break the bond with her or to get what I needed and wanted for my life. I could be with my mother, and would leave Maine for home the next day to serve as her mirror a little longer. *It's okay, I can do it.* My body was relaxing. I guess I was "inhabiting the body." Eyes clearer. Heart opening. Breath fuller.

The head was weakening from hunger. Weakening in the light of love and awareness. And it began to shrink. And this shrinking head was not a symbol of a vanquished enemy, but more a reduction of its reflection in the mirror. My dog and I peed, claiming a little ground for ourselves up there, and then I hugged my wife right on the highest part on the summit. We turned, together, and looked at the sea. In her steady and still silence, she was like the mountain . . . like the sea . . . I'd found my spot. In that moment, she, my dog, the vast ocean and sky, took me out of myself and out of the pain-bag I had been carrying for so long. Got out of my head and down into my body. The daypack seemed lighter. Everything did.

And the descent was good.

Hate

At the coffee shop where I sit most mornings, I observe people while my heart opens, hardens or is neutral towards them. In each of these random individuals, I expect there is pain enough to warrant warmth from me. I know this well. I know all impulses of compassion and love lean toward truth and anything else is a cry for help and healing.

I know this, but I always forget it. I forget when faced with experiences which insist that I remember, but I don't.

In most faces, I see nothing. I suppose I'm not really looking (too distracted by the pond over which I slouch, by the mirror in which I'm stuck—possessed by a reflection of which I never tire). In other faces, I might see sadness and worry, or see my father and grandfather, my mother and her mother. And in other faces I see arrogance, entitlement or stupidity. Sometimes I see the right kind of misery, but then the wrong representation of pain; or the right stoop or limp, but the wrong manner with it.

And then, everything can change, and they magically qualify; qualify for attention, empathy, and imagined intimacy.

But mostly, I hate. I don't actually like to hate, but it comes naturally. Being critical, angry, hateful—it is the heart *al dente* that feels like home. And that, I never forget.

A woman enters the coffee shop and sits at the table next to me; I see her softly because today I must be more sad than hate-filled. Her hands, the way her thumbs look as if they hurt, a bracelet with pink coral and silver on her right wrist, and a string of pearls wrapped around her left, which seems a quietly distinctive accessory. I look at her glasses, the thickness of them. They're magnifying lenses, but she wears them for everything, making her look a little lost in fog. She's wearing Dutch shoes and ankle socks with a pink checkered design. Cute socks. She is maybe in her forties. I feel nothing but love for this one. She is sad too, perhaps. Not particularly attractive, or is she?

Maybe something more than sorrow draws me to her. Eats her muffin slowly and sips from her cup. She is patient. Sits and has her coffee. There is no book or phone to distract her. Ring, on her left hand, which I cannot see clearly. Her shy posture tilts her a bit forward, looking around, but not intrusively. Not as if she's looking for a conversation. She simply glances around from time to time. She qualifies. I don't hate her.

Then Tall Jim comes in. I've seen him around. (I never really look at him, he's basically one of the neutrals, though he teetered on the edge of hate one time when he heard me introduce myself to someone. "Oh, you're Eyetalian," he remarked. I said, "Aren't you clever?" and turned to scribble that very line in my hate journal.) Tall Jim asks if he can sit with the woman next to me (no other seats are available). She nods, readying to leave anyway, and he says, "I hope you have a nice day." She thanks him, wishes him the same. While he's in line to order, she uses one of the small brown napkins she clutches to gather up some crumbs from the table and floor that had tumbled from her muffin. I feel reassured that Tall Jim has given her what I wanted to: good wishes in the everyday. I'm relieved. I don't have to take care of every one of them, or worry about them. There are others for that. The neutrals. Let them do it.

And a few minutes later, I revert to hating some

stranger who strolls into the café. I'm already forgetting Tall Jim and the Shy Lady and then she comes in . . .

The Fat Woman. I've seen her in here a number of times, with two young stupefied children. Dazed by her constant, animated chatter, these girls remain silent, fish-faced, eating pastries and drinking cocoa with whipped cream on top, while she puts on a show of enlightened-suburban-liberal child-rearing for all to hear and see, employing her own addictions to sweeten them into passivity. This woman is odious, a monstrous, dominating force stuffed into a small café. She could pull a plow. Her voice bores holes in my skull (but these holes do not let the demons out). When she's the only other customer (her daughters being mere satellites revolving around her colossal girth, absorbed into her gravity), I can neither read, write nor think any thoughts other than murderous ones. *Kill.* I want her gone, for the sake of the children. *For the children!* Little Christians, I'll wager, given the large, dangling crucifix sometimes hidden by the folds under their mother's pelican neck. Her display of religiosity fits with the rest of her one-woman burlesque. She does everything but cannibalize those girls. Eat their flesh and drink their blood.

Christians. God, I hate 'em.

Then two women come in and sit at the handicapped-access table I'm usually at. I like it because it's large and I can spread out. I wasn't at it this day because it was too close to her, but these women, who know the loud, fat lady, sit there and they all say hi and they ask her, "How's the new baby?" and in that moment I think, oh, maybe she hasn't been fat all this time but pregnant and this is just leftover baby weight. After all, pregnant is not fat and the hormonal changes women go through during and after pregnancies account for a lot and maybe that's what I've been reacting to. Naw. I just can't stand her.

And then she said to them, "He died."

A moment's pause while the women swallow their shock and then sob out the usual things and the lady says, "Thank you, thank you, but it's okay. He was so beautiful, and it was so beautiful the way he left us. It was really a wonderful thing how we all held him until it was his time to go. It was really . . . really something." And here, I fell into another universe, pulled by her gravity myself now. I suddenly wanted nothing more than to hear her speak again, but that's all she said, let the women hug her, and returned to the window seats where her daughters remained, and where bits of her tattered croissant passed through her heavy lips.

I forget the lesson that we are one, and we love and hurt, all of us, together. But, it seems, I love to hate, so I forget.

I forget, the way I forgot the lady I hated at that

Buddhist retreat center. Short, wide, airy-fairy hippie-looking chick, reeking of patchouli oil and covered with bells and tassels, bracelets, and buttons which proclaimed her worldviews. Her annoyance capacity was astonishing, and I had never even heard her voice or got to look into her eyes. But I hated her. Hated her excessively upright posture and her rolling narcissistic gait, her bumper-sticker spirituality, and her scented, bangled, goddess-obsessed life. I hated her auras, her crystals and her astrological sign. I hated her hair and her slippers. I hated her being. My mind spun evil all day and there were no distractions at this place. We retreatants couldn't speak, or read, or listen to music, or make eye contact with the 120 others accompanying us for ten days. I needed distraction bad.

She was also Jewish and insisted that she light candles in some horseshoe shaped candelabra every night in the dining hall. I couldn't relate to that show *at all*. Waddling up there all Jewish and holy and tribal about it. And she was always the first one in line for every meal. I was starving and, man, I hated her for that too. This lady created so much angry skull-chatter that I fantasized about leaving the retreat and going to get drunk at a local bar just so I could sneak back in and somehow frighten her to death while she slept.

This, of all things, I had developed as my individual Buddhist-retreat plan.

Then, one day, during the snail's-pace walking meditations we did when we weren't sitting and meditating, I inched by a window heading to my room, and through it saw the very woman in an open snowfield behind the monastery. She was facing the woods, her back to me, her pygmy-like arms outstretched at shoulder height, face turned skyward. She was covered in tiny birds. *What the hell?* I saw them flying to her from the far off trees while others jetted off her pudgy hands and back to the woods. A continuous loop of living motion. There were eight or nine of them on each arm and she stood there like some Twinkie, Jewish Francis of Assisi. I was stunned, stopped dead at the window, watching silent, slack-jawed.

In a few minutes she turned toward the building and headed, ever so slowly (as is the instruction) through the snow toward the rear door where I was standing in the vestibule. *Who was this now?* She had transformed in my estimation into a mysterious being that held sway over nature, which flocked to her. Wild, twitching nature. The tiny birds, still here with us in the bitter winter. Sticking it out, not leaving like their nomadic brethren. Not just any birds. These were birds of character.

She entered the door, looked at me directly and I at her (which is counter to the instruction) and then reached slowly into the outside pocket of her suede-fringed jacket. She extended a closed hand toward me. I slid my open hand under her fist and she, expressionless, let hundreds of seeds fall into my palm. The tiniest of smiles curled at the corners of her mouth as she moved on past. She revealed her trick to me as if she knew I needed something, some ritual . . . some transformational magic.

I walked straight out to the field wearing only jeans and a T-shirt, found her footprints in the snow to stand in, and with seeds in both hands spread my arms. In a few minutes, sailing in from fifty yards away, came a stream of life which landed on me, each waiting turn to take a seed and go. These babies against me, their vibrating life quivering on my open body, they blood-doped me with the current of their living energy. Not one of them concerned with which was in line first to eat. They were civilized, queuing-up like the British. Not like me, the barbarian hatemonger. They warmed and melted me, unlocked and unpacked me. After a while, in thrall, I returned to the retreat.

A few hours later, silently invited by her outstretched arm, I went up with her before dinner, and together we held the long matchstick she used to light that night's candle and we performed the sacred and the ancient ritual. Her hand shook as she placed it over mine while we touched flame to wick, and she whispered to me in a voice that I had never heard and which trembled like the tiny birds, "This is for my grandparents who were lost," and in that moment I fell again into a far rockaway of the heart. She turned to me, her eyes brimming over. She washed me with her tears and lit *my* candle that cold night. It was different from all other nights. I flew to her and she fed me. I became a convert to her rituals and to the mystery and miracle of the heart undone.

And this, even this, I would forget, if not for these occasional wailing walls I attempt to build with broken-down words.

Thank you for buying "Lunatic Heroes." This book was self-published and entirely self-financed. If you enjoyed it, please tell your friends, and even if you didn't completely enjoy it, tell them anyway . . . they might. Also, I'd love to hear your reactions to these stories. Email me at dramartignetti@aol.com, or visit my Facebook page: http://www.facebook.com/camstories.

Joe, me, Mikee and Joey
(Jackie and Carol setting up the shot)

About the Author

C. Anthony Martignetti, Ph.D., is a psychotherapist in Lexington, Massachusetts, where he lives with his wife, Laura, and their Border Terrier, Piper.

In the late 1960s, as a high school graduation gift, his mother tried to nominate him for a Pulitzer Prize, but the panel refused to accept her recommendation since nobody had heard of either him or her . . . and all he had ever written were assignments for an English class in which he received a solid B. As a result of that event he has remained, to this day, defiantly unpublished.

He got a set of Samsonite luggage instead.